Living By Wonder

Living By Wonder

Writings on The Imaginative Life of Childhood

By
Richard Lewis

A Parabola Book
in association with
Touchstone Center Publications
New York

Living By Wonder ©1998 by Richard Lewis

The author and publisher gratefully acknowledge permission to reprint the following material:

"The Silence" translated by David K. Loughran, from "Poem of the Deep Song" from *Collected Poems* by Frederico Garcia Lorca, edited by Christopher Maurer. Reprinted by permission of Farrar, Straus & Giroux, Inc.

"The lane was always the place..." by Dylan Thomas, from *Quite Early One Morning*. Copyright (c) 1954, New Directions Corp. Reprinted by permission of New Directions Publishing Corp. and David Hingham Associates.

"Magic Words" translated by Edward Field, from *Songs and Stories of the Netsilik Eskimos*. Copyright (c) 1967, 1968 by Edward Field, reprinted by permission of Harcourt Brace & Company.

"A Forest Lane Covered With Moss" and "Lotus Pool" translated by Amitendranath Tagore from *Moments of Rising Mist: A Collection of Sung Landscape Poetry* published by Grossman Publishers, 1973. Reprinted by permission of Penguin-Viking Limited.

"Thoughts While Reading" translated by Kenneth Rexroth, from *100 Poems From The Chinese* published by New Directions. Copyright (c) 1959 by New Directions. Reprinted by permission of New Directions Publishing Corp.

"Egret Dyke" translated by Yin-nan Chang and Lewis Walmsley from *Poems of Wang Wei* published by Charles Tuttle & Co, 1958. Reprinted by permission of Charles Tuttle & Co.

"Flowers and Moonlight on the Spring River" translated by Arthur Waley, from *A Hundred and Seventy Chinese Poems* published by Alfred A. Knopf, Inc. Reprinted by permission of Alfred A. Knopf, Inc., and George Allen & Unwin Ltd.

Photographs— Title Page: Dan Rous • Page 1: Carol Grocki Lewis • Page 39, 127: Helen Buttfield • Page 73: Debra Drown • Page 93: Robert Toothorap

Cover and book design: Martin Moskof

Lewis, Richard, 1935-
   Living by wonder : writings on the imaginative life of childhood /
   by Richard Lewis.
      p. cm.
      Includes bibliographical references (p.   ) and index.
      ISBN 0-930407-38-5 (hardcover : alk. paper)
      1. Imagination in children. 2. Child development. 3. Child psychology.
   I. Title
   BF723.I5L48   1998
   155.4'133--dc21   97-52573
                                                                               CIP

In memory
of
my mother and father
whose gift
was the wisdom
of their
wonder.

Books by Richard Lewis

Table of Contents

Introductory Note

Living as we do, I keep reminding myself to notice the extended process a child must move through in order to speak, and over time to read and write. And then, with increasing awareness, to listen and make sense of its thoughts and feelings. While the earth seems to be more of a global community than ever, each individual still must harness the enormously complex and solitary worlds existing within the uniqueness of a singular personality.

The essays in this book are my own means of reflecting upon the early life of this growing individual personality—and, in particular, the different strands of imaginative thought expressed throughout childhood. They are products of my observations and attempts, both as a parent and teacher, to understand and synthesize what I perceive as necessary qualities of our earliest imaginative interests and abilities.

Much of what I have included in this book was originally printed in journals and publications aimed at a variety of audiences. While some of the pieces speak more generally of childhood—and others relate specific occasions in my teaching experience—all, I hope, can be read as interpretations of the child's emerging imaginative life. All, I hope, can help us take notice again of those critical steps in childhood when the very poetry of a child's being, so alive with wonder and energy, can truly become the basis for children everywhere to construct their unique and vital worlds.

    —Richard Lewis
    November, 1997

The Languages of Childhood

Making a Language of Childhood

I've had the pleasure of watching my three children begin to speak. In every instance one can't help but be amazed and awed at this extraordinary human ability. To be close by as a child takes its first tentative steps in making sounds, in extending those sounds into single words—and finally, with unquestioned ingenuity and bravery, in joining words into a phrase, phrases into a sentence, a string of sentences into a statement, is to be embraced by heroic discovery.

If only we could remember the struggle, the daily improvisations, the waiting and longing, the taste and feel for what our speaking could and did become. If only we were witness once again to the moment we knew we had spoken, when nothing could stop us from continuing to speak. If only we might regain the excitement of newfound words following each other, repeated over and over until they were a most essential song.

But such memories are hard to recapture now. We long ago let language be part of everyday life and only occasionally do we stop to marvel at the beauty of language-making, the simple fact of speech bridging silence.

At first, as young infants, we test the strength of speech. We learn to shout and yell words, to lower our voices to whispers, to trill and vibrate, speed and slow down, accent and punctuate separate sounds. We declare independence from silence. Chasing words as they come to the forefront of our mouths, we sing them out and watch them scatter. Masters of our instrument, we tune and make ready to play with what we have to say; inventing as we go along, and the colors of words find their way through unknowns, changing a silence here, a silence there.

We are not afraid of silence as much as it buttresses discoveries of speaking—and continues to do so until, at a moment of realization, we know that we can speak and be understood. Then, we reach out for something beyond our own speaking. Curiosity moves cautiously to see what the silence is. Does a bird staring down at me speak? Does wind have words like my own? Does water, in its reflections, listen with me? A rock, a pencil, a coin, can they speak even though they now are quiet? Can I hear a voice inside a sky or what a frog is telling me with its eyes?

For the young child, stillness is the advent of something about to happen, about to be spoken. I explore stillness with children when I teach by holding up a leaf found on the ground. Without speaking I move the leaf up to the light. If I ask, "What might the leaf be thinking?" very few children doubt the sincerity of my question. Most assume that any object, if isolated from the complexity of life, can and does have thoughts. An inborn ability to give feelings to non-human things helps us early to reason that thought is not limited to ourselves. If there are thoughts in a leaf, it must want to speak. Language becomes a means of liberating the silence in things, and bringing them closer to what we want them to say—and what we wish to say through them. Our mythic tradition is based on a human ability to bring alive the languages existing in creatures, plants, moons, suns, and stars—any and all things outside of ourselves. We live in a noisy, boisterous universe of speaking things when brought to full volume.

But let us go back to a quieter quality of language-making. In an adult linguistic world where words and their actions are of such importance, we are forever talking ourselves out of the opportunity of listening to the other forms language can take. As children, we relied more on the transparency of feelings. We watched and listened not so much with the intent of speaking about things, but with immersing ourselves in the feelings we had from things. An eleven-year-old I worked with told me that "A feeling thinks by seeing and touching…" I don't know if this youngster realized what he said, but his insight was an intuited glimpse into a language experienced and not forgotten. We are animals of instinctive sensory abilities before we become speaking, word-articulating creatures. It is through seeing and touching that access arises to a language of feeling which rivets the attention on what things are. As children we do not know the names of things, but their shapes, textures, and smells. Their sensory relation to us is a language. It allows us to converse with the immediate world, and through our eyes, fingers, mouth, and nose we accumulate a wordless vocabulary of where we are.

Silence and stillness are living qualities we once knew—not as abstractions but as sensations. A student of mine, Gina, nine years old, wrote, "Shh—silence, splash the sound of the seagulls the silence of nowhere is there while the sea rocks itself to sleep." She is, in an unconscious way, recognizing the silence as if it were a language, perhaps the very language from which speaking language must initially emerge. Ngaire, also nine years old, in a piece she called "The Graves" wrote: "They are still. All over." Ngaire has made of both stillness and silence a vocabulary we can react to, substances of experience which are necessary to understanding. How can we argue when Josh, an eleven-year-old, says: "Language came from stillness, quietness, deadness." He had no knowledge of so-phisticated theories of linguistics but could with unerring ex-actness pinpoint the way he was able to converse bodily, experientially, with levels of consciousness denied us as we grow older.

I remember a distinct moment of my own childhood when a stream I was watching became more than a stream. It seemed beyond my six-year-old language to explain, because the stream was a language which included me, and I only had to listen in the unique way of a child. Many years later I came across a piece of writing entitled "Quiet Fishing," by Michael Freeman, who, when he was eleven years old, wrote:

> My float was silent and still, and its yellow and white mark-ings gleamed in my ever fading eyes. The gentle fall of dis-tant water could be heard as it pounded the stream. My mind went with the water, up and down, in and out, mov-ing forward as it went. You let your mind run away, as if swept by the stream.

The intermingling of our selves with a language encom-passing us is a human trait that allows us to connect to a di-mension beyond the confines of speaking and listening. To be aware that language is an expressive behavior throughout nature, and in objects, is not a diminishment of human language. It is, on the contrary, an acknowledgment of a broader meaning. We can, if we wish, hear and speak with untold qualities of experience inherent in the colors, shapes, movements, sounds, and smells everywhere. As Thoreau says: "A momentous silence reigns always in the woods, and their meaning seems just ripening into expression."

The complex journey a child takes through its own silence allows its silence to speak an innate wisdom rarely acknowledged as real learning. Noise of our verbalizing culture too quickly deafens what children initially understand. Their early relationship to language is a poetic one, reaching far beyond utilitarian speech. They are not surprised by speaking with the smallest bird or the most distant sun. They sense that this communication is what language was meant to be: a link to what is here, can be imagined, and has once been.

In a sweatshirt of his favorite basketball team, in sneakers softened from running so fast, in a slow and cautious voice, unsure what his fifth grade classmates might think of him, John announces how it all began: "Language came from the earth and stars." And if we are ready to go along with him, then our speaking is merely a few words in a much longer sentence.

The Wind
of the
Marigold

I remember my son, when he was two or three years old, standing on top of a large rock and talking to the trees in front of him. Every once in a while he would shout a word—a swirling of sound pressed out toward a rock, a tree, a cloud passing by. The ritual became part of his daily exploration of a small forested area where we had been staying during the summer. He had entered a period of his language development where words had taken on a magical power; heard and received by objects around him—and these objects, touched by his words, were changed forever.

My son's newfound ability paralleled what various cultures, including our own, have taken for granted: the special power of words to change and—in the most profound sense—to create. From the New Testament's "In the beginning was the Word" to the Maori "The word became fruitful; it dwelt with feeble glimmering; it brought forth night" to the Indian "On the Spoken Word all the gods depend, all beasts and men; in the Word live all creatures; in the Word is the Imperishable, the first born of the Eternal Law, the mother of the Vedas, the navel of the divine world," the word has been charged with a strength and presence that brings life. Edmund Carpenter, referring to Inuit poetry, says: "Words do not label things already there. Words are like the knife of the carver: they free the idea, the thing, from the general formlessness of the outside. As a man speaks, not only is his language in a state of birth, but also the very thing about which he is talking."

The bonding between words and their objects is one of the stunning attributes of childhood. But in very young children, the making of sounds precedes the making of words. Through awareness of sound and its power, the child slowly grasps the meaning that underlies words. Those fortunate enough to hear an infant's babbling—particularly the birdlike warbling just before sleep—are aware of the playfulness with which he experiments with sounds, rolling them in his mouth, letting them enter the silence of the darkened room, changing the silence so that he has been comforted by sounds. We cannot overestimate the importance of this period of soundmaking in a child's life. Like scribbles, they are first declarations of our inner and outer space. The making of sound must give, if only dimly, our first awareness that we are able to make something that did not exist before. It is, in the most elemental sense, a primary act of imagining.

Eventually sounds evolve into words. In whatever language they appear, they must also be, to the child, no less than magical. For words not only signify things; they are the thing itself. To say "mama" and "dada" and to see one's mother and father respond, to repeat "mama" and "dada" when they are not there and be able to have the word suggest the touch, feel, and sound of mother and father, to have an image, within the speaking of the word, of one's mother and father—how intriguing and delightful!

Octavio Paz has spoken of words as "a cluster of living beings, moved by rhythms like the rhythms that rule the stars and the planets." For the young child, they are exactly that. They are alive, not only because they are moving sounds, but because sounds influence and change the things they are about. When a child learns the word "sun" and then sees the sun, and pointing to it says "sun," a relationship has changed; the child now has the possibility of speaking to the sun, of bringing it into the context of his mind. Such naming allows him in time to speak with the sun in poetic terms. A seven-year-old writes:

> Sun, Sun do you know
> You are beams in the flames,
> With glowworms in the light
> And bright yellow red
> Sharp silver flames
> Spinning up,
> Like a big block of gold
> The sun is a very magic fellow.

Children are attracted by the rhythmic and melodic elements of language. Through chanting, repetition, wordplay, and nonsensical chatter, language not only delights but acts as a doorway to secret visions. When I was in Ghana many years ago, an eight-year-old child came up to me and as an introduction began to sing an "enchantment" song. The words made no sense, but the way she sang revealed her delight in their magical properties. I had the impression that her singing was her way of capturing my attention and bringing me into her sphere of being. She later wrote the words down:

Big ones small ones ten
and yellow red ones
blue and pinkish white ones
Mother wants a red one
give her red and red
mine will be enough
two for blue 1 boy
1 dove 2 doves
two and three
five one
give him one a blue
Pinkish is the best.

Children are often intoxicated by the sheer musical seductiveness of language. Like adult writers, they enjoy words for their sensuous appeal and their power to elicit moods and feelings beyond a word's literal meaning. Such fascination leads the child to wonderfully wild metaphoric leaps in which combinations of words and phrases create a landscape of images. The following poem—or chant, since it was sung by a child in Ireland as she rushed into the house to greet her mother—has an almost bardic quality. In the tradition of shamanism, Etain, age four, evokes the spirits beneath things:

The wind of the marigold,
The flies of the American Bird,
The shamrocks of the stones,
The Lord of the Fieldmice,
The marigold's lavender.
The marigold of the shamrocks,
The mice of the round-a-gold.

The tractors of the storm
How the wind blows
The wolves howl,
While the moon moves
Along in the sky.
The wind blows people's hats off
And blows people's dresses up.
The Lord Mayor of the Dreams,
The mari-of-the-golds,
The Lord Mayor of the Golds.

At some time in their development, most children become intrigued by the "special" word—the word which makes the window open, the door shut, the table move, the light go out. Some "special" words are made up, others are real words with remarkable powers. This too has parallels in a variety of cultures in which certain words are not spoken for fear of invoking powers which could, in some cases, kill. Edward Field's translation of the Inuit chant "Magic Words" has this to tell us:

In the very earliest time,
when both people and animals lived on earth,
a person could become an animal if he wanted to
and an animal could become a human being.
Sometimes they were people
and sometimes animals
and there was no difference.
All spoke the same languages.
That was the time when words were like magic.
The human mind had mysterious powers.
A word spoken by chance

might have strange consequences.
It would suddenly come alive
and what people wanted to happen could happen.
Nobody could explain this:
That's the way it was.

Here are two stories that reassure us that the tradition of magic words is indeed still part of childhood:

> My friend Tommy is interested in magic words. I told
> him that most magic words were backwards words.
> So Tommy said "Office" backwards and then it made
> me see things like white lightning that struck every-
> thing that was green and my wallpaper and blanket
> are green. I saw red snakes and blue snakes. And
> space ships and people pushing me. So I didn't get to
> sleep last night at all and I was almost late for school.
> —*Eric Johnson, age 6*

> Once there was a man who had some gold. What-
> ever he said the gold would do. If he said "Tree" a
> bit of the gold would turn into a tree, and if he said
> "Ham" a bit of the gold was it. Once the man said
> "World" and on his birthday he got a little picture of
> the world, and on Christmas, each birthday and each
> Christmas, he'd have a little picture of the world. One
> day on his birthday he got a silver suit: a silver pants
> and a golden shirt, and once he said to the shirt,
> "Pumpkin," but nothing happened, and he thought
> only the gold he had would do it, so he asked the
> gold for a pumpkin but nothing happened. But one

day there came to the door a green pumpkin with a
triangular nose and round eyes and a dreary halfway
smile.
    —*Christopher Pirtle, age 5*

As soon as children reach seven or eight years of age,
they discover that the word that invokes mysterious powers
can be turned to other means. It can curse, tease, ward off, in-
timidate, parody, and mock; many powers are contained in
childhood chants and rhymes. The foremost collection is *The
Lore and Language of School Children* by Iona and Peter Opie,
which verifies the existence of an oral tradition among children passed on to each succeeding generation. Words, in their
affective power, in the degree to which they protect by their
utterance our fear, weakness, and vulnerability, as well as ex-
pose the weakness and vulnerability of others, have been
made into a survival mechanism by children.

For better or worse, as the child grows, the magic of
words is turned toward aggression and defense to meet the
pressures of peer groups and the child's cravings for acceptance and belonging:

> See my finger
> See my thumb
> See my fist—
> —You'd better run.
>   —*English*

> Bug off!
> Bug off!
>   —*American*

While this use of language is common to children everywhere and is a weapon which, once uttered, brings adversaries to their knees, a fascination, even awe remains in many children for the way language operates:

> Where
> do words come from?
> The throat
> and the tongue
> work together
> and mass-produce them.
> The special liquid
> of a new-born baby's
> heart,
> stomach,
> and liver
> soaks into
> the throat
> and the tongue.
> If you carelessly speak too much
> the liquid will be gone
> and you'll become dumb.
> If you don't speak a word
> words will come out by themselves
> while you are sleeping.
> The control of words
> is difficult
> > —*Iijima Kenji, age 11*

Language, as the child discovers, can be the means to describe and evoke the magic of events and things themselves. For many, the startling sonority of words becomes its own magic, taking us into a deeper realm of consciousness and perceiving:

> Gentle as a feather
> Cat quiet
> Snow soft
> Gentle, gentle as a feather
> Softer than snow
> Quiet as a cat
> Comes
> The evening breeze.
> — *Maria Hourigan, age 11*

Fortunate is the child who never gives up the original impulse to bring forth words from silence, and words which not only name the unknown but which, in their wondrous way, take on, like the child itself, a life of their own. As Owen Barfield says in *Poetic Diction*,

> The full meaning of words are flashing, iridescent shapes like flames—ever flickering vestiges of the slowly evolving consciousness beneath them.

The First Question of All

But why?" asks the child, her eyes upon us. "Because...," we answer straightforwardly and with as precise a reason as we can muster.

"No, but why?" asks the child again and again.

Try as we do to answer these questions, children are seemingly never satisfied. Have we heard their question? Are we simply unable to find the answer they want? Why must children be so demanding of us? No matter how we approach the question they are asking, children tenaciously keep to their "why?"

We have been told that this "why?" question is nothing more than a clever device to get attention. In some instances this is true, but like the inevitable growing of a child's arms and legs, the question appears as a specific attribute of childhood. Somewhere between active speech and the worldly ability to argue for their own feelings and beliefs, children discover the incandescent virtues of "why?"

"But why," *you* might ask, "incandescent?"

What distinguishes children, or more specifically, childhood, from other periods of our lives is a duality of feelings that, by and large, support each other. The first feeling, if the child has been nurtured reasonably well, is a sense of well-being, a feeling of belonging to this time and space. Can't you still recall those particular luminous moments, such as the sound of morning outside your window, the day you played as long as there was sunlight, the snow caking on the sleeve of your jacket? Parallel to this feeling were the inevitable questions we asked—at first, only to ourselves. "Where do the sounds come from?" "Can I walk to the end of the sunlight?" "What is the snow?" In fact, these original questions may not have been asked formally, but secretly, the curious part of ourselves simply trying to understand. Let us not forget that an important part of human life is its curiosity—an innate desire to investigate something we don't yet know about. And while curiosity may have been the undoing of some other species, it has broadened the scope of our sensibility and knowledge. And all the while that we poked and pried into the things around that other question, "why?" kept sweeping over us.

"Why?" was not so much curiosity, but the nagging sense that for everything there was a reason—a real reason that brought it into being in the first place. If it snowed, why did it snow, and if it snowed because it was cold and moist, then why was it cold and moist—and so on... Somewhere in childhood we became root-diggers, possessed with the ability to surface from various unknowns into reasonable facts—only to dive down again in order to find out what was below the facts, what startling amount of ground and mud and water and darkness and heat held things together. We were not only after "truth"—whatever that meant to us—but we were digging for that incandescence of belief that, like our play, allowed us into the warmth and light of our believing. We felt related and connected to everything around—the summer day was not just an objective reality outside, but somehow, we were that summer day.

My suspicion now is that the desire to question, to separate the layers of reality into smaller and larger entities, was the beginning of a poetic understanding. By poetic understanding, I do not mean our interest in the craft of poetry. I mean, more generally, that understanding which—from curiosity, wonder, and our questions—created a bridge to the unknown, those outer and inner elements of our existence which we cannot and will never be able fully to comprehend. But it is an understanding that, freeing up dogmatic and rigid ways of perceiving and knowing, allows us to experience the endlessly evolving ways we can see and feel the world around.

What the child and our own childhood continually teach is that the answers we assume now have the potential of becoming the questions we ask later on. This "poetic" underpinning is also, I believe, the foundation of what we know as scientific inquiry— but scientific inquiry that remains in awe of its subject: nature.

One can conclude that the awe and modesty toward what we know is a characteristic we as adults inherited from the curiosity and wonder of childhood. In her book *The Ecology of Imagination in Childhood*, Edith Cobb speaks of this trait in this way:

> The ability to maintain plasticity of perception and thought is the gift of childhood to human personality; this truth is sorely abused, in our attitudes not only toward the child in society, but also toward the child in ourselves.

The plasticity Cobb cites is part of the way the child understands, and most importantly tries to understand. The spontaneous, uninhibited responses the child gives to explain phenomena are rich in the marvelous leaps of image-making typical of young children. A few years ago, when working with a class of seven- and eight-year-olds on the theme of the sky, I asked questions not unlike those they might have asked themselves.

> How heavy is the sky?
> *It's heavier than a little kid.*

> How far is the sky?
> *It's farther than India, Africa, and the North Pole.*

> What does the sky feel like?
> *Cotton, pillows, and softness.*

> How would you get to the sun?
> *You would tippy-toe.*

> How big is the sky?
> *The sky is about four inches.*
> *It's about as big as a blue whale.*

> What does the sky sound like?
> *It sounds like a bird whistling.*
> *It sounds like an ocean.*
> *It sounds like popping.*

> How big is the sky?
> *It's bigger than a planet.*
> *It's a million inches long.*

Their answers, like the questions, pull at the boundaries of reality so that what we "know" is given a richer dimension of possibility. We all can "tippy-toe"—but it indeed would be something quite special to tippy-toe to the sun. The question was taken seriously by the children ("How would you get to the sun?"). Because of the way young children think—given their buoyancy of thought and an ability to transpose one reality into another—we as adults cannot help applauding them for their startling turns of perceptive and poetic insightfulness.

I am convinced that the impulse in the child to play with questions is the tantalizing feeling that such questions give permission to be answered in a way that enriches our sense of the real. Certainly by asking "why?" whole strands of meaning are untied and let loose upon consciousness. We are face to face once again with what we may never know as a reality. For some persons, this may be too threatening or unstable to tolerate for a long period of time. But for the child, the desire to ask questions is paramount. It is the beginning of pulling back the curtain to see what is behind it, of stepping into part of myself to see who is there—or, as the poet Juan Ramón Jiménez asked, "Who knows what is going on on the other side of each hour?"

Karl Jaspers, in his book *Way to Wisdom*, speaks of philosophical thought that is not systematic, but comes instead from our desire for "awareness." Jaspers cites a child who heard the story of creation in which God made heaven and earth and quickly asked, "What was before the beginning?" He then concludes: "This child has sensed there is no end to questioning, that there is no stopping place for the mind, that no conclusive answer is possible."

Such awareness, despite our natural inclination for permanence and the exact "truth," is the raw material for poetic scrutiny. It is an awareness that touches a mythic desire to ask of beginnings their origins: "Why does the sky have stars?", "Why is the moon so cold?" and "Why is the night long?"

The mythmaker that is the child scans the horizon of his or her knowledge and wonders why things become what they seem, creating a picture of the world that, like all of life, is forever changing and evolving. Perhaps if, as Wallace Stevens said, "Poetry is the imagination of life," then it is we, the imaginers of poetry, who continually are asking, first as children and then as adults, questions we pivot a sense of being upon. Our earliest cries, cravings to speak, and earliest marks on a page—each of these experiences brought another way to ask another question of ourselves and of the life around. Such questions, whether they could be answered or not, expanded us, for they brought us closer to being able to live with what we don't know—which in its way illuminates our inquisitiveness and fragile attempts to frame what we feel and hear and understand, despite our ignorance.

Gaston Bachelard, in *The Poetics of Space*, said, "In poetry, non-knowing is a primal condition..." In asking "why?", we ask the first of all questions. And still, like the child, we ask "why?". Its warm ferment of thought has not left us; even after so many days and nights have passed, it still lingers. Are we its question? Or has it, persistent to the end, become the reminder of what we always want to know?

"But why?" the child asks, like a bird calling in the spring—again and again.

Infant Joy

If you look at Pieter Brueghel the Elder's great sixteenth-century painting *Young Folk At Play,* you will see more than two hundred children engaged in eighty different games. Aside from the extraordinary visual impact of the painting, there is, if you allow yourself to hear it, a great din of children's voices—yelling, teasing, and laughing. This is no different, of course, from a contemporary playground filled with children moving everywhere in the midst of their most important undertaking: play.

If you look more closely at the Brueghel painting, you find a few children with gentle smiles on their faces, smiles that express the good pleasures of play itself. Certainly, you might remember those absolutely pure moments when your playing felt like you were at the very center of the earth. You had become the axis on which the rest revolved. Why not smile, since what you were doing was as delicious as drinking a long-awaited glass of cold water on a hot day?

When my children were very young, during summer vacation in the country they used to disappear after dinner with the neighbor's children. Sometimes the only way we knew where they were was to listen for their laughter. And such laughter: wonderful glissandos of delight rolling over the fields. It was a sound, high-pitched and vibrant, that if you didn't know it was coming from children, could have been a wondrous new species of bird excitedly singing.

Nothing was more awkward than reminding my children and their friends that it was getting dark and perhaps they should be coming home. There would be a few words between us, during which their laughter would stop—a compromise agreed upon—and then their laughter would rise up again into the treetops and remain aloft until they came home. In this connection, I am reminded of William Blake's poem "Nurse's Song":

> When the voices of children are heard on the green
> And laughing is heard on the hill,
> My heart is at rest within my breast
> And everything else is still.
>
> "Then come home, my children, the sun is gone down
> And the dew of night arises;
> Come, come, leave off play, and let us away
> Till the morning appears in the skies."
>
> "No, no, let us play, for it is yet day
> And we cannot go to sleep;
> Besides, in the sky the little birds fly
> And the hills are all cover'd with sheep."
>
> "Well, well, go & play till the light fades away
> And then go home to bed."
> The little ones leaped & shouted & laugh'd
> And all the hills echoed.

When one thinks of a child's laugh, one is confronted by the enormous variety with which children laugh. Perhaps, as we get older, our laughter begins to find its character—and its tone. We recognize another person's laugh as we recognize the way the person speaks. But with young children, the modulations of their laughter are still part of trying on different sizes of feelings, attitudes, and expressions. Just the other day, while waiting in a crowded airport, I heard a child laugh—and everyone, including myself, turned around to look. We looked not because we were concerned but because the laugh itself was riveting. Like a bell, the child's laugh rang through the crowd of people and brought another reality. I thought: no matter how chaotic things are, there is the laugh of well-being and good-honored innocence. It seemed like the feeling we once had when we played vigorously as children and all that mattered was play. As Dylan Thomas describes in his story "The Peaches," "There, playing Indians in the evening, I was aware of me myself in the exact middle of a living story, and my body was my adventure and my name."

So too with the child's laugh at the airport. The child invited us into his world, just as his laugh emanated from his body. Because young children are fully in touch with their sensations, and the intellectualizing characteristic of later years has not yet occurred, their laughter, like their play, springs from their whole body.

But prior to the peals of laughter of children playing after dinner or a child's hypnotic laughter in a crowded airport, there is another bodily response in children that is an enigma to experts on child development: the smile. How do we learn to smile? What is its meaning? What we know, of course, is that the smile is a common expression in infants—almost from birth. Is

this first smile the beginning of a sense of humor, or has it more
to do with a child's pleasure and contentment? Surely the smile
of the Inuit child in this lullaby expresses the latter:

> LULLABY
> It is my big baby
> That I feel in my hood
> Oh how heavy he is!
> Ya ya! Ya Ya!
>
> When I turn
> He smiles at me, my little one,
> Well hidden in my hood,
> Oh how heavy he is!
> Ya ya! Ya Ya!
>
> How sweet he is when he smiles
> With two teeth like a little walrus.
> Ah, I like my little one to be heavy
> And my hood to be full.

We might even, as does William Blake, call this kind of
pleasurable smile the embodiment of joy itself:

> INFANT JOY
> "I have no name:
> I am but two days old."
> What shall I call thee?
> "I happy am,
> Joy is my name."
> Sweet joy befall thee!

Pretty joy!
Sweet joy but two days old,
Sweet joy I call thee:
Thou dost smile,
I sing the while,
Sweet joy befall thee!

Learning to smile, like learning to walk, must be one of our first great linkages to what exists around. We might speculate that the smile, whatever its meaning, is the infant's way of communicating to someone else. Be it a mother, father, or stranger, we respond in kind when the child's open face slowly begins to change into a smile, and the urge on our part to continue to make the child smile is contagious. How many of us have become instant buffoons, getting on hands and knees, barking like a dog, squiggling our faces into a talking ice cream—literally anything to prompt the smile to show itself on the child's face once more!

But the smile, for all its tranquillity (and perhaps mystery), is only a prelude to a larger burst of joyfulness when the child finally laughs. It is a laugh that can come from the child's simply being lifted out of her crib and gently tossed about in another's arms. Oh, for us to be that child again—absolutely relaxed and trusting, knowing that each time we will land safely in a warm cushion of arms and comforting words. The whimpers, gurglings, and hardly-able-to-catch-her-breath laughter the child shakes with as she feels the luxury of moving way, way up high—and then all the way down—is a laugh to greet the physical universe. Issa, the Japanese haiku poet, has this in mind when he writes:

> Crawl, laugh
> Do as you wish—
> For you are one year old
> This morning.

Indeed, the ability to laugh is, as suggested in this Apache Indian myth, essential to living:

> The creator made man able to do everything—talk, run, look, and hear. He was not satisfied, though, till man could do just one thing more—and that was: LAUGH. And so man laughed and laughed and laughed. And the creator said: "Now you are fit to live."

Within the very structure of the new laughter is a particular ingredient which, for the child, is of utmost importance if he is to move on to further levels of laughter. We might call this ingredient the human gift to play with the expected and unexpected. When small children are tickled, for example, they laugh, sometimes with great hilarity. The hilarity stems from what James Sully, in his *Essays on Laughter*, calls "attitudes of indefinite expectancy." The child does not know when he is going to be tickled next—and the waiting for the touch of fingers on his stomach becomes a moment of wondrous expectancy. This is also true of the laughter-provoking elements when we play peek-a-boo. When will mommy show her face again?—and when she does, often disappearing, there she is—like magic, all over again.

To laugh at the moment that wasn't quite expected is at the core of turning the expected into the unexpected. In other words, we take reality and change it—turn the world topsy-turvy just enough so that it is "funny." I suspect this making of "nonsense" out of what is supposed to make sense is one of the great lessons of play—the child's growing aptitude for transforming.

What a fascinating education in humor it is to talk to a group of four- or five-year-old children and tell them about the day I once saw chickens walking down the street with umbrellas, in order, of course, to keep from getting too much sun, and every time it rained, the chickens would flutter their wings and wobble down the street, and their umbrellas would wobble down the street, too.

The image of an incongruous series of events sets the children giggling and laughing, full of expectations of what will happen next—when the sun comes out again. The genius of the child to feel comfortable with the anthropomorphic, to the extent that anything can have ears and eyes, can talk and have feelings, opens up vast possibilities of humor. But we must remember that what a child will find absolutely humorous may not necessarily strike adults with much hilarity. Here are a few thoughts of kindergarten children about a special imaginary worm they adopted for their classroom. When the children shared these thoughts with each other, there were many moments of instant and empathetic laughter.

> This bus is going to the zoo. This bus goes very fast.
> The school bus is going to go to the garden, make a
> turn, and park. The worm is driving the school bus.
> —*Shamarie*

> The worm opened his door
> and saw his flower.
> He lost it but then
> he found it again.
> —*Omar*

He didn't know how to get up so he made a squiggly turn.
—*Sarah*

He's squiggling because he has an itch he can't scratch.
—*Christopher*

One can assume that without play the child cannot learn to balance the various realities of her world. Certainly, without play that sees things in a humorous, slightly off-centered way, the child is unable to make sense of a world that (we know all too well) is definitely not a stable mechanism of consistency and contentments. Much of a child's sense of humor, and some of her most boisterous laughter, is created when she tries to make sense of one of the most complex issues in her life: adults.

GROWNUPS
Grownups are silly,
They never drink coffee
When it's served
To them.
They just talk
And never drink it
Until it's cold.
Isn't that silly?

I haven't grown
Since I was five
I haven't grown at all—
Grownups are just getting shorter.
—*Marc Duskin, age 10*

A TEACHER
A teacher's got a temper
Like a bull.
He growls and roars
Like a tiger,
He stamps and gets mad
And sometimes he's glad
He did it.
                    —*Bruce McGregor, age 11*

I have read the teacher poem many times to children of all ages—and the sheer excitement of hearing another child challenge authority (and often so true) brings children to their feet, yelling: "Read it again, read it again!" And each time I read it, the room fills with more and more laughter. I realized at one point that sometimes when I read this poem I become a bit like the teacher: my voice deepens, and my eyes bulge somewhat. This for the children is equally as mesmerizing as the poem, for I have become, without realizing it, a clown. In the mind of every child the world must sometimes be played out as a circus so that they may find a suitable equilibrium within reality. As Margaret Lowenfeld says in her book *Play in Childhood:*

> Buffoonery is an essential element of good education. To be able to enjoy the unexpected, to perceive the incongruous, and to welcome the grotesque, is to start out with a good equipment to make sense of so strange a world as ours.

Just as the best of Zen teaches us to laugh, so too do children teach us to not take seriously all that is serious. R. H. Blyth, Zen translator and scholar, says:

Laughter is a state of being here and also everywhere, an infinite and timeless expansion of one's nevertheless inalienable being. When we laugh we are free of all the oppression of our personality, or that of others, and even of God, who is indeed laughed away.

One evening I went out to have dinner at a restaurant. I sat near two children, about six or seven years old. Amidst the refinement of a beautifully set table, the voices of these children were about to alter the mood of the setting:

> *First child:* Why did the girl blush when she opened the refrigerator door?
> *Second child:* Because she saw the salad dressing.

Grins, a burst of giggles, and a warm laugh from everyone within hearing—and the world, for the moment, had somehow righted itself again.

We grow from our laughter as much as from our seriousness—and the child, discovering the magic of humor, finds a new plateau from which to view his experience. What new expectations await the child who has begun to laugh, if only with his eyes. What unexpected moments have yet to happen. What a time we had when our playing was a smile over the face of our lives.

Trying On
a Hat

When most of us were very young, at one time or another we put on our parents' shoes and hats and went to look at ourselves in the closest mirror. We walked around the room pretending to be our mother or father or someone else much bigger than we were. My father had a sailor hat he wore when he went fishing and I remember putting it on and feeling very proud—as if I were my father or the captain of a ship. Even now I watch my youngest daughter, who is barely a year and a half, trying to put on her colorful woven hat from Guatemala. When she succeeds, she struts around the living room like a bird with new plumage. She can't tell us what she feels but her expression is one of delight.

Just the other day, I walked by a sixth-grade classroom in a school where I teach. A student wearing a long piece of shimmering yellow fabric casually draped over her blue jeans and sweat shirt informed me that she was "The Sahara Desert." She swayed, dream-like, back into the classroom where her classmates, studying African cultures, were also costumed in a colorful array of scarves and hats. I was reminded of the time when, while teaching, I would playfully offer children my jacket or my tie, even my wristwatch or my glasses. The obvious transformation in their demeanor, their instant characterization of adults, was often hilarious.

You don't have to go very far to find the comic tradition in full bloom in children. They will take advantage of anything within arms reach to be funny. Parents can testify to the times their children rummaged through an off-bounds closet or a set of drawers to find just the right mismatch of clothes to dress up in—and then with almost faultless precision, to act out a day in the life of their family. No detail is left out, from Mom's dislike for the cat to Dad's penchant for talking on the phone—everything we thought the children hadn't really noticed is scrupulously absorbed and edited to its most humorous. The command of timing, of the right gesture for the right moment is quite often devastating, and—if you are not one to be intimidated—full of laughter.

When we think back, we are reminded of how much time in our childhood we pretended to be someone else, of the hours spent fantasizing and trading places with a host of characters who in their realities frightened, intrigued, or baffled us. All we needed was to put on a top hat (and anything else suggesting a character), and within seconds we had let the curtain of our imagination rise. Whoever we wanted to become we became, and it didn't matter whether we had a live audience or not. The fun was in letting ourselves assume a personality and acting it out, silently or publicly.

Where did this gift for the dramatic come from? Is it part of our cultural inheritance or an innate human ability? I suspect the latter, because long before what we now know as theater, the mask and the animal skin had been used to disguise and assume the personhood of a god, a spirit, or a crea-

ture of the wild. It was our human way to appease the unknown, to heal wounds, to reaffirm our place with what, like
ourselves, was also alive.

And this belief in the magic of costume and adornment
grew out of our childhood desire to play, to make believe. One
wonders about how play itself evolved within our species, but let
us speculate that it grew with a maturing intelligence. Play was
our secret weapon when we tried out possibilities beyond codi-
fied behavior. Thinking fancifully for a moment, I imagine play
may also have been found by accident when a group of children
gathering branches showed them to their elders. The elders may
have thought the children, holding branches above their heads,
had turned into animals—the same antlered creatures they inter-
acted with every day. In a striking moment, the appearance of
one thing had become something else by changing what was
worn. Illusion had begun.

The child in the yellow shawl and those wearing their parents' jackets or hats are doing what children do anywhere in the
world—trying out as much as they are trying on, what other realities feel like. Imagination is the license to see what a hat, a jacket, a shawl is, and children become actors in their own emerging
lives. It takes no special talent to do what they are doing since
they are following one of the oldest rituals of childhood—inventing, through playing, the characters each is becoming. Their play
is both rehearsal and the real thing: a stage which keeps turning
into something else.

Learnings and Rememberings

The Pulse of Learning

It was one of those warm summer evenings. I was on my way home when, just at the entrance of the park where I had been sitting, I saw three small children chasing fireflies. It was getting late, but I lingered for a moment to watch them. The children were completely involved with what they were doing: the sweep of their arms as they tried to close their hands on a firefly's humming light; their bodies arching forward when what escaped them suddenly appeared a few feet away; their excited whispers sifting quietly around us. Then quite unexpectedly, one of the children, sure that she had caught a firefly, came running to her father nearby—and opening her hand, proudly showed him what was inside. Both she and her father looked, but there was nothing except her bare hand. No matter, off she quickly went to her friends, dizzying themselves in their leaps and hoverings, trying to find out what it must feel like to have particles of light so close to them.

A moment, perhaps—but the poetry within it wasn't about to leave me. I was touched by the way the children were totally absorbed. For the briefest time they seemed to be an example of something learned in which no part was absent. Everything—senses, mind, and feelings—was in a balanced state of concentration; and to separate these elements would have been to take from these children a perfectly natural way to discover what they had not known before. The unity of this triad is the essential ground for this kind of learning—a learning that is most evident when children play. I keep trying to discover how this learning can be a recognized and cultivated part of education. Not an easy task, since education today is more intent on separating our learning capacities than in bringing them together.

How stifling it is for many children in our schools to find after kindergarten (in some cases before) that the prerequisites of getting ahead in school are to divide play from work, imagination from fact, feeling from truth. How confusing it must be for children to be told that their senses (hence their bodies) are not where they learn, and that real learning takes place only in the citadels of their intellect.

What unfortunately is true for the majority of children is that to succeed in school it is best to become a passive learner. One must not invent or discover, but imitate and acknowledge. One must not question and doubt, but accept and obey. Such a contract with passivity has spawned an educational dilemma that educators are hard put to solve: how to relieve the contagious boredom affecting children (as well as teachers) once learning has been separated from the taproots of curiosity and imagination, from the sources of learning in which children think and feel, as well as play and work.

With our emphasis on scholastic learning, we have denied what children already know about learning—not as an intellectual definition, but as an intuitive understanding of their own world. For most children, the instinct to learn, actively and enthusiastically, is most evident in their earliest years when they first begin to walk and talk—and as importantly, to play. What happens, if a supportive human bonding is reasonably intact, is the development of children's natural desire to learn—to move with their own internal impulses to understand and to survive in the world evolving around and within them. These impulses—and these learnings—are not "schooled" as much as instinctual; they emanate from children precisely because they are crucial to their existence, not just physically, but as a consciousness becoming aware of itself. In other words, a sense of inner and outer, of thought and feeling, of body and self, is working through children in an extraordinary fashion; so that, just as a seed assumes the form of a tree, they assume the form of their human aliveness.

The important question is how to bring instinctual learning into school. What can be done to instill learning as an active—even passionate—concern? How to unite the broken triad?

For clues we have to go back to the qualities of our own earliest learnings—to the time, just as with chasing fireflies, when our learnings were our hands and feet, the entire experience of our bodies, sensorially probing the world around. We have to find moments that were not defined as learning, but whose meanings are still with us: the time we walked in the snow and listened intently to our footsteps, or the time we fell down in the ocean and couldn't catch our breath. We have to remember that when we are very young learning is not linear—it is a learning, as the novelist Eudora Welty noted in *One Writer's Beginning*, that "stamps you with its moments. It isn't steady. It's a pulse."

Because boundaries had not been constructed, everything was to be listened to—taken in, so to speak—in the safekeeping of awareness. Knowledge was not a subject matter broken into unconnected thoughts, imagination was not different from reality, and play was the work we knew best. We were sensory beings related to the languages of ideas and feelings. We knew something by the way we felt about it.

And it was the strength of feelings that allowed us to empathize with much around us. When we listened to stories, we became the wind and the sun and the serpents and the heroes. We could believe with Katherine, a six-year-old, when she wrote: "Long, long ago people could see and feel the stars and sky because the sky was down so that people could touch and feel it."

Katherine is telling a truth that children—like ourselves—learn most deeply and personally when thought is joined with feelings and they experience the totality of their bodies responding to ideas. Thoreau suggested the importance of how "thoughts must live with and be inspired with the life of the body." In a similar vein, it was Emily Dickinson who said:

> If I read a book and it makes my whole body so cold no fire can ever warm me, I know that is poetry. If I feel physically as if the top of my head were taken off, I know that is poetry. These are the only ways I know it. Is there any other way?

Dickinson's question prompts me to reply that what is crucial to learning is to see it as poetic—that we must restore to learning the artistry within it. We must bring back to teaching the deepest respect for the art that is teaching, as well as the recognition that the artistic act, when it succeeds, incorporates the triad of learning, so that mind, body, and feeling are one entity. In his book *The Aims of Education,* Alfred North Whitehead stresses the need to make this triad of learning paramount to education:

> You must not divide the seamless coat of learning. What
> education has to impart is an intimate sense for the power
> of ideas, for the beauty of ideas, and for the structure of
> ideas, together with a particular body of knowledge which
> has peculiar reference to the life of the being possessing it.

We must, as Whitehead states, become more aware of the "life" of the learner—aware that one's thoughts and ideas are manifestations of life, and pulsate, as do all living things, within the fluidity of the entire body known as the human being. I cannot help noticing that the descriptive phrase "human being" is itself active, and intimates that which moves. To capitalize on this possibility means that the exchange, as well as the making, of our ideas and thoughts, is a bringing together of all that is alive in ourselves and others, so that our feelings, our minds, and our bodies are no less than a personal integration through which the expression of life moves.

I wonder now whether the children are still chasing those fireflies in the park. A number of days and nights have passed since I saw them—and I suppose they have found new fascinations. Yet I am quite sure that in the memories of the three children, the pale phosphorescent glow of lights which darted mysteriously away is still moving. I am quite sure that in each child something new has begun—and continues—to fill them with the excitement and pleasure of what there is to know. The shadows of their enlivened spirits—the poetry of their knowing—tells us much about how we might learn, with them.

The Child's Remembering

Reflections on Poetic Meaning and Thought

I have always been fascinated by children's play. In particular, I am fascinated by children's abilities to fuse with the object of their play. When a child plays with a toy fire engine, for example, she lies on the floor on her stomach, pushing the red fire engine. The pushing of this small toy is not all, however—for the child also makes the sounds of a wailing siren, the guttural sputtering of its motor, and if you listen carefully enough, the excited conversation of the firefighters on the way to this imaginary fire. For the moment of play with the fire engine, the child becomes the object of her play.

The gift of becoming other than what we are—letting ourselves be transformed by the object of play, or transforming it so that we become that thing—is at the very core of our imagining self. I suspect that without this play, the ultimate existence of the imagination would be in jeopardy.

For me, as a teacher concerned with nurturing the imaginative life in children, especially through poetic and mythic thinking, the power and importance of play are crucial. Because our educational institutions from kindergarten through college make little or no attempt to integrate the process of play (or the imaginative process in general) into the curricula of learning, children as well as adults have little opportunity to experience (if not re-experience) the degree to which childhood play and all its capacities are not only relevant to adulthood but crucial to expanding consciousness and thought.

I have become aware of an interesting phenomenon when working with junior high school students (approximately eleven, twelve, and thirteen years old). I often choose themes such as "the earth" to frame new learning. Using myth, poetry, and our conversations, I elicit from them a sense of the earth as it was millions of years ago. What makes these students alive to a different way of thinking is not just the sharing of thoughts about the earth, but my bringing in tangible objects such as an eagle's feather, the skeleton of a sea horse, a fish fossil, or a living flower. Their astonishment is with the object itself as an object. Suddenly isolated within all our words, questions, and probings is an object that can be looked at and, more importantly, imagined upon. We play with such questions as:

"What does the eagle see when it flies above the earth?"

"In the sea horse's mind, can it imagine how the sea began?"

"In the oceans that filled the Grand Canyon, how can this single fish survive as a memory of that time?"

"How does the color and shape of this flower remind us of flowers that lived before us? Was there a time when there were no flowers?"

What emerges from the junior high students is a slow but persistent need to play with ideas; to become the small child they once were, playing with a feather or a flower, and entering into the world the feather and the flower represented. Something else also occurs: as we play around and through these objects, the students surprise themselves and their classmates by the things they see. Living in an urban landscape, they are startled by the details of their observations of what the earth was like millions of years ago, or the drama of the sea's beginnings. None of them have been there physically, but the act of imagining enables them to envision worlds impossible to inhabit—except through the imagination.

THE FEELING OF THE EARTH

My feeling as the earth since sleeping in the winter
when rain came down and the wind blows would be
like small stones landing on me and the clouds are
like blowed through words, like speaking.
—*Alex*

The roots hear different things on the stages they go to
reach the earth. On the lower stage they might hear
animals or insects travelling through the earth. On the
higher stage they might hear rain or the earth forming.
—*Linda*

HOW DID IT ALL BEGIN?

There was all yellow. There was nothing but a meaningful glow. It was like that of a spirit, or that of a harmless
creature. And it was in another dimension, not the kind
that we know of today. There was no day, and there was
no night. But strangely enough, there was a sun and
there was a moon. But they were not necessarily the sun
and the moon, they were more like their spirits. And they
all helped in making an unknown dimension glow, and
make strange things happen.
—*Tanaka*

> Swirling, twirling
> bright colors.
> Then came this low humming sound.
> Human.
> Then a high pitched sound.
> There it was—
> the Earth formed by little specks.
> —*Guy*

The question that arises is how the children, in connecting themselves to some object or image-as-object, remember in an unconscious fashion, (as only the body can) biological memories of our collective past. As we play, we uncover those deeper recesses of thought and feeling which are our human past in relation to the prehistoric stirrings of the earth's beginnings.

Even younger children make connections to the deeper recesses when, for an intense moment, they become the object of our focus:

> The water inside my body is admiring itself. It is in my fingers and the palm of my hand. It's admiring, it's beautiful, deep and brilliant purple with touches of pink, blue, red, and green. They talk about easing my muscles, because they can do this whenever they want to. They are very happy about their home in my hand.

> When I drink water, it goes to my hand, but when the water enters me it changes colors, like gold, violet, grey, etc. When the new water touches the old water, the colors blend in. That means that they like each other and if they like each other then they talk. They

talk about beauty and other beautiful things. This is
when I feel happiest.
　　　　　—*Olivia, age 8*

The wind grew
colors and then
it vanished into
the eyes of the
big night.
　　　　　—*Lynette, age 9*

These children are able to touch the poetic semblance of
things. By remembering not only with their intellects but with
the fibers of their inner feelings and intuition, they bring into
being what we know but rarely have access to—except in the
unconscious language of dreaming. If we define the poetic as
a letting go of the hard and fast rules of routinized reality so
that objects, events, and experiences are placed in a different
context, then the play of imagination is the activity that gives
the initial impetus to an innate poetry of learning.

This poetry establishes a relationship between ourselves
and what exists and has always existed. Rilke said, "The task
of the poet is to connect the remotest past with the furthest future." The "remotest past" is lodged in each child as a member
of our common biological heritage. As Lynn Margulis writes in
her book, *Symbiosis and Evolution*, "Every form of life on
earth—oak tree and elephant, bird and bacterium—shares a
common ancestry with every other form…" Even the language
we speak has a biological ancestry, not unlike what William
Carlos Williams has written: "Earth, the chatterer, the father of
all speech."

As the child plays, he is entering a consciousness that has access to what can be remembered only in play. This remembering is vast, for it includes not only personal experience, but the child's link to sensation and memories beyond his capacity to explain or understand. The child has become a listener who speaks through himself what has been heard but cannot yet be defined—a knowledge unconscious but awakening.

In *Psyche and Symbol* Jung said that "the child had a psychic life before it had consciousness." In his paper "Analytical Psychology and Education," he states: "The unconscious is the ever-creative mother of consciousness. Consciousness grows out of the unconscious in childhood, just as it did in primeval times when a man became man."

To verify the unconsciousness, we must allow children to feel at home in play. Even more, we must encourage the play of their imaginative resources not only in childhood but as a growing source of insight and expressiveness throughout their lives.

For a number of months I worked in a fifth-grade classroom in a section of New York surrounded by streets that promised little else except more streets. In that classroom we made "the sea" the object of our play. I carried with me a short poem by the French poet Guillevic:

> For want of an ocean
> There is your palm
> to look at.

There was a child in the room who was shunned by her classmates because she daydreamed so often. I am sure her daydreams were, to her, "the palm of her hand"—transforming her world from its unconscious state to a consciousness of something seen and experienced. One afternoon she wrote:

> The moon enters the water.
> It splashes the water
> in different colors.
> It forms a dance
> round and round.
> Suddenly a piece of
> the moon flies off.
> The blackness of the
> earth dances beautifully.
> —*Catherine*

Catherine's gift was not only the poem but the play of her imagination that let her become the moon and the earth. She had become aware, and her awareness embraced the subtle balance of the unconscious and the conscious, what we know and don't know as they bring us closer to the nature we are.

Wallace Stevens speculated that "the poem is a nature created by the poet." But might the poem be the nature in which our entire self exists, and which we must enter, as the child who played, to find what lives there? As Kerry reminds us, we ourselves might be the memory of a larger remembering that unfolds through us.

> Poems in your mind—
> They've always been there
> since the first day of birth.
> —*Kerry, age 9*

Acting
Out
Daydreams

I once had the opportunity of working with children in New York schools, in which I organized a series of workshops around the idea of dreaming. I was not interested in using the dream in any therapeutic or analytic way, but in simply recognizing it as a manifestation of human thought that had significant ties to the poetic and imaginative process.

Part of my desire to explore dreaming with children came out of my reaction to the rigid thought processes impressed upon them through their schooling life. Factual ideas, the classification of concepts as right or wrong, sterility of feeling and perception were what children, for the most part, experienced in school. Little attention was paid to a childhood in which dreaming was related to a fluid inner consciousness that, like playing, was a necessary means toward understanding and expressing the meaning of experience. The love that small children have for topsy-turvy nonsense, their delight in believing in the "lives" of inanimate objects, their leaps between the fantastic and the real—were simply not, at least in school, seen as nurturable elements of their personalities. It seemed a fascinating challenge to make dreaming a legitimate way for children to move through learning and into the equally important realm of imaginative expression.

One discovery I made, after organizing several groups of children ranging in ages from seven to twelve into a series of weekly dream workshops, was how accessible their dreams were to them. Our initial discussions around what dreaming and dreams were elicited excited responses—as if a room filled with treasured images had been opened. Nightmares were the most interesting to share, not only because they were frightening, but because as events, they pushed possibility to its extremities.

Eventually our discussions moved into painting, drama, movement, and writing—and the rich vein of image-making tapped by dreaming led to their interior world. This, in turn, allowed them to explore the "interiorality" of practically anything of interest to them: the dreaming of stones, of the sun, birds, frogs, and water. We took a Japanese haiku poem by Chiyo-ni,

> O butterfly,
> What are you dreaming there,
> Fanning your wings?

and imagined, through movement or drama, what the butterfly might be dreaming.

The delicate line between the actual and imagined, the point at which a poetic idea takes root, were a part of each workshop. A window in the room where we worked became the source of powerful associations which lay just beneath the surface of immediate perceptions. This short prose piece by one child was, for her, a first attempt to see beyond the concrete sense of the window:

> The window turns into a big glass monkey with five eyes, fourteen arms, one leg and half a tail and the monkey does a wild dance then turns back into a window again. Now when you look out of the window there's a lady with a dog and the lady has no head and there's a man that's pulling something by a rope, but there is nothing at the end of the rope…

What became apparent during the course of the workshop was that we were not speaking only of the kind of dreaming that we do at night. To look at a window or to transform oneself into a dreaming butterfly is to dream consciously—to do the one thing often forbidden in school, to daydream. If daydreaming could be experienced as a crucial step in approaching the mythic and poetic sensibility within as well as the flow of intimations, images, and feelings that make up the inward state, then perhaps we were on our way toward giving the children a greater sense of what was available on an expressive and imaginative level.

As the children worked through their daydreaming experiences, it was obvious that most people daydream a good deal in waking life, and daydreams exert their own kind of stunning symmetry. They literally take one through boundaries of thought and feeling impossible to move through in more rational moments. The satisfaction of daydreams is their intimate secretiveness—as if only the dreamer, at that moment of dreaming, is possessed of the ability to do what her daydreams are doing. Dylan Thomas says it wonderfully in this selection from the book, *Quite Early One Morning:*

> The lane was always the place to tell your secrets; if you did not have any, you invented them. Occasionally now I dream that I am turning out of school into the lane of confidences when I say to the boys of my class, "At last, I have a real secret."
>
> "What is it—what is it?"
>
> "I can fly."
>
> And when they do not believe me, I flap my arms and slowly leave the ground only a few inches at first, then gaining air until I fly waving my cap level with the upper windows of the school, peering in until the mistress at the piano screams and the metronome falls to the ground and stops, and there is no more time.
>
> And I fly over the trees and chimneys of my town, over the dockyards skimming the masks and funnels, over Inkerman Street, Sebastopol Street, and the street where all the women wear men's caps, over the trees of the everlasting park, where a brass band shakes the leaves and sends them showering down on to the nurses and the children, the cripples and the idlers, and the gardeners, and the shouting boys; over the yellow seashore, and the stone-chasing dogs, and the old men, and the singing sea.
>
> The memories of childhood have no order, and no end.

The following writing by a six-year-old child echoes that of Thomas, reemphasizing the fact that just as daydreams are a flight through imaginative realms, so can the daydreamer fly:

THE GIANT

Sometimes when I play in the garden with my Brother
Andrew and when I climb up the Pear tree I seem as I
was a giant. I feel as I could get onto my roof and
stretch my arms in the sky and get to clouds and play
with them, and I could be across the road without
waiting and pick up people that looked like ants, and
could pull up swings, and houses, and then tell my
mother.

—*Jeremy Roberts*

The dance generated by letting the children "move with"
daydreams was often remarkable. As they danced, their bodies were no longer moving by the rules of strict time and gravi-
ty; they could invent gestures that lifted them into unusual
configurations and patterns. Their daydreams suspended their
conditioned way of expressing themselves. New feelings for
language began to emerge:

> Falling, falling, falling, up, up, up, falling, down, down,
>   down, down, over, over,
> blow, blow, blow, melt, melt, push, push, push, crash,
> crash, twist, twist, fall, slide, slide, push, crash, melt, melt,
>   squirm, squirm,
> shake, down, down, down,
> sleep, awake, sleep, awake, turn,
>   turn, crash,
> melt, roll, flat, pull, move, down, *dead*.

The children began to sense a correlation between the
impulse to express something and the ability to daydream the

object of this expression into being, to allow themselves a free-floating period of time to gestate their feelings and ideas. Then they were able to take human situations occurring around them and draw them into their worlds—and from them invent, or daydream, other situations. One "situation" happened one day in class outside our window—a terrible screech of brakes and the sound of breaking glass and metal from a car accident. We all rushed to the window to see two cars locked together. After a discussion comparing times we personally had been involved in a car accident, they all sat down and wrote "daydreams" based on what had just happened. Nicola, who was eight years old, daydreamt this:

> The bird crashed into a rock.
> The flower crashed into the ant.
> The water crashed into the sink.
> The pencil crashed into the paper.
> The pin crashed into the pin-cushion.
> The clock crashed into the time.

As the months passed, we experimented with evolving dream "dramas" that could be taken outside and performed in the schoolyard or in the park. We asked the photographer Arthur Tress to film what took place, and to make still-picture dramas, which were developed and made into a series of "dream books"—which could be read as a sequence of unfolding images and interpreted in endless ways. I suspect that as the children grew closer to playing with images, or letting the images play upon them, the feeling for images became more acute. They recognized that images and image-making were a way of making sense of the world. In a society strangled with prefabricated television images, to lay claim to the images of one's own is no mean feat. There is a poem by Mazaki Kiyonori, a Japanese child, which speaks eloquently to this point:

THE EYE IN THE SCENERY
I ran in the sky.
Shooting stars are wrapped with the cotton of the
    clouds.
Thousand and thousand of lights.
In the scenery of my mind, they follow me as I run in
    the sky.
A darkness passes through my mind.
The natural sky disappears into red.
In the scenery of the sky, the sun is sleeping in the
    universe.
The future calls the sun.
Round lights,
broken and scattered lights,
the universe is deep inside me.

The reality of the "universe within" is what we were trying to make apparent. If we give children a deeper sense of the language that speaks within them, of the streams and rivers of thinking that run beneath their outward commentaries, of the magical fictions and poetry that make up their inward life—then the workshop would have its value.

But let me say that through focusing on dreams and giving children license to express their dreams, many instances of children bringing to the surface deep fears and hauntings occurred that obviously were part of working through traumatic and unresolved dilemmas in their own lives. My role was not that of a therapist, but to acknowledge the children's dreams and to use the energy of the dream as the raw material for the shaping of their imaginative and artistic vision. The following story speaks of the powerful mythic quality that emerges when a child is given encouragement to tell the story of a dream as it was felt and imagined:

> Once there was a man and he was out in his ship all alone and it was night. And suddenly all the waves came bigger and he looked up at the stars and they came bigger. He felt scared. The stars came very big and then they burst into big snowflakes. The snow-flakes began to open very slowly and out of the snow-flakes came witches and ghosts and all sorts of scary things. Then all the snowflakes turned very little, and then they changed back into stars and the stars went little. The witches' ghost and all the other things came down to the man and began to shake him. It was real-ly a nightmare and just then he woke up and his wife said, "Take this drink of orange and have a game of cards with me and it will pass out of your mind." And all the time it was night.
> —*Jacqueline Wright, age 7*

As the workshop drew to a close, what was so fascinat-ing to observe with the children was their belief in the multi-plicity of realities that naturally intersect in the complex process of perceiving. They began to question, in a healthy way, the fabric of knowing. They slowly, if not without frus-tration and impatience, started to experience the fusion of seemingly contradictory ideas as they turn into metaphors.

They became alive to the ways dreaming opened up new perspectives out of which their experience took on a unique personal and expressive dimension.

> Sometimes I think it's all a dream. Well I mean....Just say it's the beginning of time and you're dreaming your life....You've not been born yet though. So maybe when you're really born maybe a thousand years later or something....Well...have you ever...like when you see something and you think you've seen it before...Well maybe you have in the dream of your life you had at the beginning of time when you were just a seed.
>
> What I mean is you're dreaming your life right now. Whatever you're dreaming—you're dreaming but maybe in 1960 or 1950 or whenever you were born that will happen again because it was only a dream before—but now it is real.
> —*Jessica, age 10*

*The Story
the
Child Keeps*

There are some children who carry their stories so close to them that they can hardly stop talking; there are some who carry their stories so close to them that they can hardly speak. Some become restless and impatient as they listen to another's story because their own stories are struggling to emerge. And some children, their stories still hidden from their view, do not always understand what a story is and does.

In a classroom in New York City not long ago, a child was frightened by a story I told about a tree that could listen and, with its ever-changing leaves, talk to us. At first, Joel did not want to believe what I was saying—I was challenging a reality he had carefully fashioned. Then one day, when he realized how the story could allow him the life of his own imagination without asking him to forfeit everything he knew of this world, he wrote:

> It's amazing how the wind moves the trees.
> It moves my mind also.
> When I look at a tree
> I feel brave and bold.
> When the wind blows through the trees,

The trees whistle in tune
for beautiful music.
As I listen, I smile.

Another child, Michelle, in a classroom in a different part of the city, was all acceptance as I told her class a story about a magic flower that could become all the colors of the sky. She received my telling of the flower's story without any trace of doubt, her open face responding to every gesture of the story. One day, she took one of us aside and confided her reaction to this kind of story. "When you imagine things...they start to grow," she said. "If you love them, they love you back. When you have an imaginary flower, it grows in your mind and you can dream it always. And no one can take that away from you."

In both instances, the children begin to see the mind as more than a mechanical operation for correct answers. They sense our inward ability to understand who we are as well as the nature of the world we inhabit. The "imaginary flower" Michelle speaks of has the organic properties of a growing flower; and we can dream it into being. From inside ourselves, we grasp and create the story of this flower or any flower. Because it is we who are dreaming this story, it becomes ours forever.

For many children, there is little opportunity to express realizations like those of Michelle and Joel. An entire childhood can pass without ever realizing an inward life. What is often experienced by these children is a one-dimensional self, eager to survive but ill-equipped to use the imagining self as part of that survival. How often we hear of children whose daily routine is made up of attending classes in which little attention is paid to the welfare of their inner lives. After school, they go home and sink despondently in front of television sets that whir away into the night. The television set has become a mythmaker for children in our culture; the television set has become a substitute storyteller.

What myths does television teach children? Much of what they see is advertising. Children, like the adults in our culture, want the things that are advertised. An awareness of pleasure that can be obtained by experiences or events like stories—which are not quite "things"—is absent from many children's lives.

Furthermore, much of what they see in between advertisements has to do with violence and death. Imagine the effect. One of the most subtle and difficult parts of childhood is the realization that to be alive, we also have to die. A culture such as ours, in which violent death has become a predominant fixture, instills a despair in children. One might ask if any of these children were ever read to by a parent, teacher, or other caring adult, or if there was any effort to help the children get closer to the stories they are telling themselves and would like to tell us, no matter how awkward they may seem to our adult ears.

Over the years, I have been able to work with children who were not aware of their own inner lives, and consequently, of the stories within them. I am struck by certain similarities in the way these children perceive themselves and the world around them. Excessively afraid, they exhibit hostility to their peers and to adults. Their fear expresses a lack of connection to the inner self and to an outward community. This inability to move comfortably between different temporal and spatial experiences is expressed by a dogged realism: Things can only be what they should be, not what they could become. These children are caught in an arid rigidity where imagination is suspect. Rigidity of thought is reinforced by our societal distrust of the usefulness of imagination. Not until the children are given a chance to slow down and sink into themselves—by someone who encourages listening in the child—is renewed response in the child brought into being. I am startled when we ask children to reflect on a simple object, to imagine what it feels like to be that object and to write a story from its standpoint. This small story—by a nine-year-old boy imagining he was a typewriter—slowed the author down just enough to be amazed by how much he could hear of himself inside the story of an object:

> Every now and then somebody sticks a piece of paper in Me. I don't get one thing that is I don't see why they keep clicking Me and turning My noise and changing My best color. Every time they are done with me they would always take the paper out of me. And there is one thing wrong with Me that I do not get. I keep on hitting Me.

By imagining himself as an object, the child uncovered the sense that something important had gone wrong in his world. What he wrote was not a metaphor by an adult to explain his problem to him, but rather, his own story from his sense of meaning.

Adults need to make it clear to each student that he or she has the tool with which to create meaning. That tool is the imagination. Once children recognize the imagination as something powerful within themselves, they live more fully.

Most children listen to other stories when they become conscious of their own, when they understand that what they have to tell is equally pertinent to the world as the treasure house of stories that have preceded them. Making children aware of their own stories is as easy as engaging them in conversations about how they feel, what happened on the way to school, or what they talked about when they last saw their grandparents. Because we tend, in our highly accelerated culture, to distance ourselves from the details of everyday experience, stories of daily events seem insignificant. As we allow less time for conversing, it isn't surprising that children find it difficult to savor stories passed from one person to another. Instead, we are captivated more by large-screen cinematic dramas, underlined with music and fast-action editing.

To counter this, I once asked a group of children to look, for a period of days, for the stories that lie just outside their apartment windows. Tony, who was then eleven years old, wrote a series of daily entries called "From My Window," from which these two excerpts are taken:

> Tuesday: I see only two bags of garbage and about 20 pigeons. I see a boy looking out of a window. Then the mother comes and tells him to do something. I see that the sky is cloudy and it looks like it's going to rain. I see that a lot of smoke is coming out of our chimney. I see no lights are on and I see pigeons on our window. I see it is not maybe going to be a good day.

> Friday: I see pigeons flying around in circles around and around. I see people having a Birthday party and that the people are having a cake and taking pictures then they dance then they see as the person opens the presents. The person is a lady. She gets towels, perfume, powder, earrings. I think it is her husband who gives her the ring because they kiss then some go little by little.

When Tony read his "story" to the rest of the class, I remembered how, in my own childhood, I would spend hours staring out my apartment window. Like Tony, I saw from this secret vantage point a world unfolding before me—a story, if you will, that was constructed by my imagination. I remember the delight on Tony's face when I explained that the story he wrote was one that he had made. Unlike stories that come from television, this story was coming from him—his observations and understanding. Though this is obvious to us, children are not sure they have the ability to see and construct something uniquely their own. Added to this is their lack of faith in their own imagining. When children realize that they not only have the gift to see inwardly but to take their inward vision, transpose it into a story, and share it with others, extraordinary growth can occur.

One child, when asked where his stories come from, said, "When I make up a story, it comes from the corner of my eye." Perhaps this is how we all find our stories—extending our imagining self through the corners of our eyes. What we see and hear is the person we are and feel ourselves to be. It is the play of imagination which leads to a sense of the unknown, to images and thoughts not yet envisioned. Because of the premium put on pragmatic thought—on how much we "know" as opposed to what remains "unknown"—children are afraid to imagine. The imagination itself becomes another unknown. What better way to confront this dilemma than literally to make the unknown a part of our story—as this child in speaking about where stories come from:

> The earth got its stories from listening to other planets.
> And they got their stories from the stars. And they got

their stories from the sun. The sun got its stories from the darkness, and the darkness got its stories from making them up.

What a pleasure it is for children to know that they are the source of this "making up," and to observe concurrently that throughout all of nature, things begin and can become something else. A story is simply about what happens. If so, stories are everywhere, both inside and outside of ourselves.

When Joel said, "It's amazing how the wind moves the trees. It moves my mind also," he was speaking to all of us about the story that each of us keeps. Within everyone, child or adult, an elegant narrative of a story exists between ourselves and the life around.

That story is a place of possibility in which we take part in a world that enhances, enlivens and offers us something with which we can identify. Through that identification, we grow. We become more than we are. We learn how to get from here to there. Though a story may challenge what we already believe about our world, ultimately, it is through stories that spirit is nurtured.

In a time when children can easily lose the birthright of imagination, we must find new ways to help children to the sources of the stories they urgently wish to tell. Each time they speak their stories, they establish once again the fertility and importance of their imagining selves.

My imagination is a nuisance and a help. Whenever I try to figure something out my mind just goes off and I'm in another world, but somehow the story in my mind answers my questions.
—*Justin, Age 9*

The Solitary Voice

Children
and Their
Solitude

In the intermediate school where I have been teaching, there is a room on the first floor set aside as a museum. I sometimes use this room for my classes with the children, and one particular day I came early. As I opened the door, I saw a child of about ten or eleven years walking around the room, looking intently at the exhibition of photographs on the wall. She didn't see me, or if she did she gave no notice, and while I stood at the door, I could see her looking at each picture with a depth of curiosity and knowingness that seemed unusual for her age. The photographs were portraits of urban children and adults in their homes and in the streets and had, in their way, the same intensity of feeling she was bringing to her looking. There was, in the interaction between herself and the pictures, an animated space, a speaking that comes when two separate thoughts converge in common understanding.

I felt awkward standing at the door—as if I had intruded on her conversation—and so I quietly closed the door and left. In the time since that incident I have often thought about the child, and can still see her moving from picture to picture, absorbed in the intimate bond she had established. What was it that made the moment linger in my mind? Did she, as she bent over or stood on her toes to get closer to a picture, represent for me an attitude of serious thought, unusual and unique? Or had she, unbeknown to herself and without pretense, given herself to the pleasure of becoming deeply involved with what she was seeing, an involvement that anyone in our fractured and hurried world would envy?

As I reflect on the image, my fascination had to do with both her seriousness and her involvement—and something else as well. She touched the part of me that is at the core of our learning: the solitude of ourselves speaking with ourselves. We might legitimately ask, where is the solitary part? Is it located in a place within our minds to which we retreat when realities press too strongly against us? Is it accessible at all times, or is it available only when certain conditions allow it to exist? How do we know that solitude exists in us at all?

What I would like to propose will have no basis in scientific fact. It is purely a subjective sense of what might be a human characteristic often taken for granted, or slighted as unimportant and intangible. It has a great deal to do with the child looking at those photographs or, to put it more personally, with the child we all were (and might still be) and the children we work with.

Change the scenario for a moment. Imagine a day when, as a young child, you were wading barefoot in a stream or in the ocean. You had no intention of swimming, you were content to walk in the water. You were with a friend or you were just alone. In any case, you were enjoying the feeling of the water touching your feet. And as you walked, you felt a sense of yourself that had nothing to do with the strict boundaries of learning as experienced in school.

You felt, if I might presume, a connection to your own sensations, and these sensations in turn moved inside your thoughts. Somehow, thought and sensation were entwined and you were aware of hearing yourself speaking, murmuring, humming—even listening. You were alone, yet in the daylight of your thoughts you were conversing with a larger personhood than only yourself. What is this personhood? For each of us it is different. It is a feeling of being within the texture of life itself.

Such feelings are what playing must have been when we were very young, when we and the object of play were content to be within the enclosures of playing. Yes, we were learning the nature of our solitude when we played, for like a cocoon around ourselves, our play taught us to transcribe feelings through imagining. Thoughts became the silken threads of enclosure, delicately woven in and through our sensations. We were beginning to see and feel the experience of what we were—and the valleys and hills of an inner landscape stretched beyond ourselves. As Gaston Bachelard, the French philosopher, said: "Childhood is at the origin of the greatest landscapes. Our childhood solitudes have given us the primitive immensities."

In this region of childhood solitude, we have stored a vast collection of feelings, images, and sensations—some so small and subtle that only when we have the opportunity of listening to the solitude can we recall them. Herbert Read said in his book *The Innocent Eye*: "All life is an echo of our first sensations, and we build upon consciousness, our whole mental life, by variations and combinations of these elementary sensations...." If true, then there is every reason to use our solitude to reach the inherent knowledge in each of us. The question is how to find "solitude" and use it, particularly within teaching.

In attempting to nurture the imaginative experience in schooling, I have found that we reach the solitary place in children by creating an image that allows them to travel to their solitude. For instance, while pursuing the theme of the sea with a group of children, we spend a great deal of time listening to the world inside a shell, actually imagining ourselves as the shell. Or while studying the earth, we might imagine that we are a seed or the roots of a tree inside the earth:

> I can hear the trees crumble,
> I can see the stars,
> I can see time flowing by,
> I can see the picture in my eye.
> —*Emilio, age 9*

What is important—aside from the child's deepening understanding and empathy for the root, the sea, or the shell— is how these aspects of the natural world allow the children to move into their own world, peopled by the multitudes of feelings and sensations. To immerse ourselves in the existence of something other than ourselves often enables us to touch and express the inner world, just as Andrew did when he wrote about his pebble:

> My pebble dreams.
> My pebble dreams of love.
> My pebble's hearts fly in the air.
> My pebble feels the wind.
> My pebble lives in a shell.
> My pebble wakes up, his dream has ended.
> —*Andrew, age 10*

To enhance the region of solitude through teaching is to make apparent to the child the extent and richness of his own interior world. Given education's present overemphasis on validating what is factual, solitude can help children realize the importance of their own thoughts and feelings.

I am amazed that when children are aware of a solitary space within, they are more engaged in the possibilities of their childhood. Their playing, daydreaming, fantasies, curiosity and wonder, questioning and, ultimately, learning are that of children who have not lost their childhood in the homogenizing of learning and growth. They are children who have, like a well planted tree, allowed their roots, their interior world, to be the nourishment of their lives.

> ROOTS
> I would hear myself climbing inside. I will hear the insects walking and when it rains I hear myself drinking, drinking to stay alive.
> —*Shontal, age 9*

To teach toward our solitude is to use the experience of solitude as a synthesis of our complex world, a mediating point out of which a personal clarity can eventually emerge. To find an expression from solitude is to find a language through which we can hear ourselves—and listen to others. To build upon solitude is to be confident that our imaginative vision is limitless and, like Thoreau, we can say:

> The landscape lies far and fair within and the deepest thinker is the farthest traveled.

Or, just as the child looking at the photographs in the museum must have felt, we can also say:

> I didn't know there was another me in the world.
> It seems that every time I smell a flower I see myself.
> —*Jill, age 10*

A Season
for
Listening

Autumn comes in on its own:
the morning frost, the yellow and red against green, the flock-
ing of birds ready to migrate. We listen differently—the sound
of the branches and leaves suggesting all too soon the winter
ahead. We are, like some tree-dwelling creatures, getting
ready for the longer darkness, watching and gathering into
ourselves the last of the blossomings, the final scents of decay
before the snow arrives. It is our season for listening—not
only to the chilly spirals of wind, but to the movement of our
thoughts.

And inside classrooms there are children—rummaging
through their thoughts: storing their endless jotting of information, seeing the iridescent shape of a daydream, holding a sensation flickering close by, scribbling into memory something
that happened a few minutes ago. While autumn might take
from us the obvious appearances of growth, the nature of a
child's thought is multiplying in all directions. There is so
much in their thinking we can't see but remember in our own
thinking when we were young. Then our minds, unlike the
season around us, were still planting, still taking in not only

what had to be learned, but the vast accumulation of what we wanted to know and already knew, those multitudes of ideas and feelings and images which we somehow intuited to be just ourselves.

I remember the wonderful aura of knowing that there was something distinct inside my thoughts, that, for better or worse, was my world. I also remember the disappointment of realizing that this world—these thoughts, generating effortlessly more and more thoughts, were not to be a part of what I was in school for. Yes, I watched the squirrel and learned to bury a part of the world I might have been able to harvest later.

This need not be so. A major insight in educational thinking is the possibility that we are now able to give to children a way their inner worlds can be expressed and appreciated. In the last two decades (and certainly in isolated situations before that) the arts (in collaboration with schools and teachers) have demonstrated that a poem, a dance, a drawing, or a play gives to children an entry to the world that is themselves. What the arts already possessed was what the child already knew: the ability to play with and transform the experience of ourselves. The discovery that the arts are a bridge to a child's thoughts and feelings has opened up the greater possibility that learning, in its most fundamental sense, is truly an act of imagination. That such possibility exists brings both teachers and artists into a new relationship.

The crisp, cold nights of winter make us listen beyond the settled quiet to the first, almost inaudible, sound of snowflakes falling against the windows. So too, beyond talking children, the speaking of their thoughts, waiting to be heard.

Emily's Tree
Imagination and
The Soul of Learning

For some time now I've kept a pencil picture on my desk of a tree drawn by Emily, a ten-year-old I worked with in a public school in New York City. After many years, I still remember how, with great concentration and effort, her thin shoulders bent over the top of her desk, she carefully made her drawing.

Drawing was important to Emily because, despite great personal hardships, she needed to make things—particularly with words and images. Luckily she discovered that by making poems and pictures, she could express what she was feeling. She also discovered that drawing was not something school had time for. When I first met Emily, her only pictures and poetry were secretly pushed into the lower part of her desk along with crumpled papers of long-forgotten homework assignments.

Like many children, Emily's interest in making things was not unusual. Like most children she enjoyed playing. From earliest childhood, she assumed that one way to make sense of things was to play them out, to change things until a pattern emerged that was pleasing—even if no one understood what

she was playing at. Knowing Emily, I'm sure she was comforted by the textures and shapes of small things: the fresh rush of
air when she opened a window, the scraping sound of her
teeth as she ate a piece of bread, the lightness she felt in her
arms after it had stopped raining. To her, these were signals,
messages conveyed to herself that she was alive.

Emily never wanted to share or speak about her feelings
in school. In her mind, school was a place to perform what
she had been asked to know. Yes, she was learning—but only
in isolation from herself. Her imagining, the pleasure she
found in making things, she did in secret somewhere else.

I recall, long before I worked with Emily, how a group
of children in another school once challenged me on the
"imagination." "But Richard," they vehemently protested, "it
won't get you into college or get you good grades." I stood my
ground and explained why they need to imagine, how the
imagination is what we are, and how without it we don't
know ourselves or each other. By the end, I don't think the
youngsters accepted what I was saying. I worried that the
children had been indoctrinated with a point of view which
denied them access to a quality of life, of living.

Why is this form of knowing so difficult to bring into
mainstream learning? Why must Emily and those questioning
youngsters hide what they feel? Why has education, despite its
concern for the mechanics of literacy and computation, too
frequently made the recipients of its teachings incapable of re-
lating to what is alive and meaningful in themselves?

One way to view these questions is to look back at how
Emily made her tree. The "concentration," the power of imagination to focus many thoughts and feelings into a single image
of a tree. The tree, initially within Emily, becomes a tree out-

side of her. The imaginative skills at work are not to be marginalized, for they are our human desire to link us to what we are.

The imagination as a consolidator is not to be confused with a more common view of the imagination as an illusionary process, or (as some would have it) as "making believe." The former is a process through which we create a perceptual bond between ourselves and everything outside of ourselves. This perceptual bonding is a biological activity in the same way the eye, the tongue, the ear, the nose, and the fingers enable us to see, to taste, to hear, to smell, and to feel. Without imagination, it would be impossible to experience the infinite qualities of our senses. Imagination is an organic process stamping processes with the same individuality as do our finger-prints or the modulations of our voices.

By making her tree, Emily was activating the biological impetus of her imagination. She was fulfilling an instinctive need to project one's inner imagery onto some outer object. The need to say what I see, feel, want to know or don't know, is a biological necessity as much as eating, loving, and the act of breathing. Whether we speak with musical sounds, bodily movements, written words, spoken voices, or visual images, we are linking ourselves to the first imprint, the first significant gesture made by human life to speak and be known consciously.

Last year, in the same school Emily went to, I worked with Jose, another ten-year-old, who in a moment of attentiveness and concentration, looked at pictures he had just painted of the sky and told me what he saw:

> The wind is pushing
> the sky
> through you.
>
> .....

> One sky is like being in it
> so this sky is a nice sky
> to the family that is in my heart.

> I imagine that it will always be there.
> ....
> When you spin around
> and spin around
> it looks like

> you're flying
> with the sky.
> ....
> When it rains
> there's a smooth wind by you.

> The wind loves its body.
> .....

I was reminded how, as imaginers, as biological beings, we too interact, interchange, fuse, and penetrate the ever changing processes of nature. We feel in the deepest part of our imagination, as did Jose, the sky moving through and flying with us, and the wind as a body loving itself.

Are the electrically charged pulsations of thoughts like the immense energy the wind propels itself with? Is the mind's circuitry like the intricate network of forces in the smallest particles of living matter? Might our imagining be a mirror of what we observe in nature—the shaping of the world around us? Can we view the imagination not as an abstract appendage, but as a primary source of consciousness, capable, as Jose was, of perceiving "the family that is in my heart" where the sky "will always be"?

If we revise our understanding of the imagination so that it is the basis of learning, we will look at Emily's tree differently. By the outward realization of her inward image of a tree, she produced a spark, a filament of energy, which made her a participant in her life. She made a bridge of the imaginative act to a portion of a sky that can be brought to her heart, not as an abstraction or metaphor, but as the physical reality of her aliveness.

If we are to educate the young to value only the final products of their learning, we have lost the soul of what learning is: a never-ending means to understand the unique sense of life each of us inwardly has been offered. The making of a tree by Emily may not be a whole curriculum, but it is a choice to retain the energy that makes up our inner world.

The Speaking
of
Rainbows

Friends meet in middle age and inquire about a mutual acquaintance: "I wonder what became of her?" From the other end of the spectrum, parents place upon their children, overtly or subtly, the expectation: "What are you going to be—what are you going to become?"

What is implied is that as we move along the course of life, we "become." We emerge from one state of being into another—from childhood to adulthood, from dependence to independence, from ignorance to knowing. There is, in our intellectual understanding of "being," a sense that "becoming" has to do with the development of life in general—the seed in the ground becomes a tree, the afternoon becomes the night, the rain falls and becomes a puddle. We assume that "becoming" is a natural constant, despite the fact that much of the time we are not aware or do not wish to acknowledge the change in ourselves. We assume that for something to change, it must shed what it was. In our case, we equate becoming mature and adult with giving up the child we were. This is true—but the danger here is that we give up something of childhood which, because of societal and attitudinal pressures, is pivotal to change and "becoming" as we get older.

This was brought home when a teacher friend of mine gave me a drawing of a rainbow by a seven-year-old child named Rachel. What was exceptional was not the rainbow Rachel drew, but what she had written boldly across the top half of the picture: "A Secret Language Is a Rainbow."

Thinking about this notion, I found out a number of things. She had exemplified what is "heroic" in childhood, namely, the innate ability to see deeply into things. This is not an attribute taught to children, but the intuitive gift accompanying the growth of childhood. The ability to see deeply—the awareness of children to perceive the spectrum of possibilities within something—in Rachel's case is the ease with which she links speaking (and language-making) with a rainbow. A sensory and intellectual immersion allows her to experience the rainbow, not as a material object, but as a living being, a part of herself. She identifies herself with the becoming of a rainbow. It becomes her rainbow when she tells us that the rainbow is "a secret language." Does she know the secret? Or is the secret her search for what lies behind the wonderment and meaning of what is alive?

In the transformation of the child into the adult, what Rachel has heard should not be lost. As we humans grow, we should bring the sense of Rachel's rainbow. Our technical skills are astounding and in themselves extraordinary. But these accomplishments of our mechanical sensibility should not blind us to the need of retaining the childhood of knowing. Perhaps our historic desire to nurture the poetic, mythic, and artistic capacities in ourselves is the human longing to keep alive the child's playfulness and imaginative energy.

Now more than ever, the balance must be struck. While we might invent the definitive light bulb, the ultimate weapon, or state-of-the-art sound—happily for us, we will never complete the knowledge of awe. For as many rainbows as there will always be, there will be untold numbers of children looking at them, and in one crucial intensity of understanding, these children will feel the rainbow speaking a language, whose secret is the lingering amazement of our being here.

Within Nature

The Blossom
Shaping

In a wooded area in Hingham,
Massachusetts, a group of fourth graders are sitting alone or
in clusters of two and three under trees, on top of rocks,
among patches of wildflowers, watching the drama of the natural world unfold. It is a spring day, and the air is clear, with
gusts of a spring wind to remind us of its presence. The children have small manila envelopes where they have been
keeping their poetry and prose on small pieces of white
paper, folded in half to give the feeling of a book. The children are quiet, except for their occasional laughter as they get
used to the calm and intensity of their surroundings.

I walk around the group, marveling at their attentiveness. Many children are simply looking, waiting for that moment when what they are looking at speaks to them. I
watch Paul, who is writing his thoughts on a piece of paper.
He looks alternately up at the sky and back to what he is
writing—immersed in a conversation between himself and
the sky. A little later, I go up to him—and he shows me
what he has written:

> The wind was soft and silky.
> A cloud alone
> calmly drifts away.
> A bird by itself flies away.
> A cloud appears
> and helps me home.

I comment to him how he has really captured the moment—the sense, also, of himself within the movement and rhythm of nature. He understands, because Paul has been part of a fascinating project taking place in the South School in Hingham, a suburban community outside of Boston.

The purpose of the project has been to introduce fourth-grade children to Chinese culture and thought. It is an intensive ten week immersion in Chinese ideas, from calligraphy to the uses of bamboo, wood, and clay. From Chinese food and the role of yin/yang in nutrition, to the discussion of Buddhism, Confucianism, and Taoism, and the creating of art and poetry based on Chinese aesthetics. The project has allowed participating teachers and children to experience another culture in an exciting and productive way.

I worked with children in the classic traditions of Chinese poetry. While I myself do not read and write Chinese, I am a great admirer of the arts of China, and have published a book for young adults entitled *The Luminous Landscape: Chinese Art and Poetry*. Using this book as a basis of my work, I began exploring with the children the ways the Chinese poet perceives the natural world and fashions a poetic statement. My overall intent was to help the children to write, using the Chinese poems as a guide, their own personal expressions of the natural world.

Paul's understanding of the movement and rhythm of nature—particularly the sense of himself—emerged out of discussions I had previously had with the children. We had spoken initially about *ch'i*—the Chinese concept of the spirit that resides in all elements of nature. This belief stems from the larger belief of Tao—which sees nature, be it mountains, rocks, streams, or trees, as alive. What brings about an individuality to these elements is *ch'i*—the spirit residing in them.

Before the children had taken up their positions, I spoke not only about looking at objects in order to see beneath the surface—but also about fusing the feelings of the object with the feelings of themselves. In other words, to come close to what one Chinese poet said: "Heaven and Earth live together, and all things and I are one."

I read the following poems by the classic Chinese poets Zhu Xi and Mei Yao-chen, respectively:

THOUGHTS WHILE READING
The mirror of the pond gleams.
Half an acre in size.
The splendor of the sky,
And the whiteness of the clouds
Are reflected back upon themselves.
I ask the pond where I can find
Anything else as pure and transparent.
"Only in the springs of the water of life."

A FOREST LANE COVERED WITH MOSS
Summer rain makes the forest muddy.
Slanting sunbeams reflect again and again.
Pure green, no wind ruffles it;
Let the spring grass smile!

What was important was to give permission to the children to do something many had done, unconsciously, since early childhood—enter into the natural world as they would enter their home. One inherent aspect of the imagination is to "feel" the life in things and to intuit the personality of things in terms of human characteristics. For the children to know that one could "Let the spring grass smile" only verified what they discovered in solitary moments of playing, when they and the grass were entwined. This Taoistic thought is apparent in some of the children's poems that emerged that day, and in subsequent meetings.

> A glittering shimmer runs through the trees,
> through the brush, through the leaves.
> A big white blue circle is in the sky,
> above everything.
> A small pond reflects it all.
> Moonlighted paths sing tunes as they hum
> through the forest, over trees, logs, and berries.
> —*Abby*

> Water
> Smiling to me
> It looks like a rainbow
> of colors under the sea.
> The moons waving to each other
> How beautiful it is.
> —*Erin*

> I see the moon
> reflecting on the water.

It is swimming very fast.
—*John*

The latter poems speak empathetically of water. During the project, I tried to use the Chinese term for landscape painting, *shan-shui*—and its translation, "mountain-water picture"—as a guide for enlarging on such empathy. To the Chinese, mountains and water are symbols of great spiritual significance, as in this epitaph to the Chinese painter Yuan Meng-hui:

> In the mountains
> One sees
> Human-heartedness.
> In water, wisdom.

One of the first things I encouraged the children to begin, back in their classroom, was a scroll (a strip of adding machine paper) on which they could draw a journey through any imaginary landscape of mountains and waters. Poems, images, and thoughts could be written on the landscape, not unlike the calligraphy (and most poems) found on classical Chinese landscape paintings. As one unrolled the children's landscapes, written in the corner of a sky or a hill or by a stream were observations of waters:

> A cool, refreshing river
> flowing down a hill
> like a steed galloping
> down a mountain.
> —*Alison*

The boat was alive because it was going across the water. The waterfall was alive because it was moving down. The mountain was alive because the trees were moving on it.
—*Brad*

I'm sitting next to a waterfall. It's right before the sunset. It was cold. A never ending river. Some laying down. Desert of waterfalls.
—*Jane*

Water is the carver,
the healer,
and the life-giver
of nature.
—*Danny*

Aside from helping these children, through Chinese poetic thinking, to respond and write about the natural world—as they instinctively are capable of doing—I was hoping to give them tools for seeing deeper into the phenomena they took for granted. Much of Chinese poetry and art concerns itself with delicate and sensitive observations of fleeting actions of nature—which, because of their brevity, we do not see.

Egret Dyke
Swoop! The egret dives into the red lotus blossoms.
Slash! He breaks the clear water into waves.
How handsome he looks in his new-born feathered silk
Proudly balanced on the old raft, a fish in his beak...
—*Wang Wei*

Lotus Pool
Unafraid of the dashing rain on the pool,
Enameled leaves conceal each other.
Colorful birds suddenly fly in alarm,
Their rush scatters the sunset glow on the ripples.
—*Mei Yao-chen*

I asked the children to capture observations in a single image. I encourage them to let the image be more than enough for our imaginations to find poetry in—and thus they saw:

A snake sliding across
the ground like a baby
crawling across the room.
—*Bruce*

A rabbit raced
through the forest
while the snow
came sprinkling down.
—*Melissa*

The boat sails on the water.
The trees still have dewdrops.
—*Shannon*

Such observations heightened our attentiveness and gave us entry to the meditative feeling of Chinese poetic thoughts. We read the following prose selection from the Chinese painter Jie Zi Yuan Hua Zhan—and considered the moon as alive as ourselves:

…a figure should seem to be contemplating the mountain; the mountain, in turn, should seem to be bending over and watching the figure. A lute player plucking his instrument should appear also to be listening to the moon, while the moon, calm and still, appears to be listening to the notes of the lute.

We talked a great deal about the moon, especially the magic of its light. Because Chinese poetry has a painterly quality, the cadenced and rhythmical brushstrokes of words etch the subtle modulations and effervescent movement of light as it finds its way to us. We listened and watched as we read this poem by Yang-di:

> FLOWERS AND MOONLIGHT ON THE SPRING RIVER
> The evening river is level and motionless—
> The spring colors just open to their full.
> Suddenly a wave carries the moon away
> And the tidal water comes with its freight of stars.

I asked the children to write from themselves right where the light is shining—feeling its every gesture as though feeling their own body walking through the forest at night. They remembered their own experiences of moonlight—and then on their small pieces of paper wrote:

> The moon is rippling
> Just like the water is.
> The moon is reflecting them
> looking at each other.
> *—Sara*

When the moonlight touched that lovely flower it
springs up in a sudden whirl of happiness.
—*Samantha*

The moonlight is shining. A poem. If you can read the
poem in the moonlight, it will shine on the universe.
Then everything all around us will be a poem. As it hits
the water, I see both communicating. A piece of reflecting moonlight.
—*Joe*

One hopes that the profound insight of Taoism concerning
the interdependency of our lives within nature will not be lost.
For these children, through their poetry, to feel their commonali-
ties with trees, birds, grass, mountains, and water is not only an
experience of literature, but a way of perceiving their own lives.

As they watched the unraveling of events that spring
morning, they understood how Joe could say "Everything all
around us is a poem" just as the Chinese poet Zuan Mei said:
"Only be willing to search for poetry, and there will be
poetry..." They expressed their own identity—with the deepest
life-forces in everything that lives—not only discovering the *ch'i*
of their own words, but the *ch'i* of what they were writing
about. Such discoveries are the grounding for bringing literature
and experiences closer. One child, Philip, said it as succinctly
and simply as any Chinese poet when he wrote:

When I touch the flower, I feel the blossom shaping.

A Simple Branch
Will Do

Haven't you sometimes felt, as you ride in a car, how quickly removed the landscape is from yourself? Hills, fields, trees, rocks, and lakes appear momentarily in lustrous presence, then merge and disappear into each other. Our eyes catch a glimpse of this or that facet of the landscape and by the time we have finished our journey, what we saw was how quickly nature moved away—retreating into "pleasant" (even beautiful) scenery and a casual backdrop to having arrived somewhere.

Looking from the window of a plane—seeing what cultures before us craved to see—the earth and the sky brought together in transcendent colors and shapes—we end our flight unaware once again of the landscape and skyscape we sped through with mechanical efficiency.

Watching a television program about the "natural world," we become removed from the physicality of the landscape. Visual images pass by—and while we are astonished by the minutiae of what we had seen, the experience becomes a "parenthesis" in the forward motion of our lives and the onslaught of images.

It is no surprise that we see "nature" differently now, because of the tempo at which we move through it. It is also no surprise that many children, living in both rural and urban settings, are part of a life which virtually prohibits them from encountering a sense of nature—not just a television image or a car window away, but as something here: around us, in us, a biological process profoundly integrated with and linked to us.

Without knowledge of the nature within, there is imminent danger for children—and adults—of being unable to feel the life of thoughts and imagination: an ability as crucial to inner ecology as forests are to the species inhabiting them. The link between our human self and our water self, our leaf self, or our animal self is not a romantic notion of nature—but one which has ageless roots.

But how do we cross the chasm of thinking caused by the brilliance of technology surrounding every aspect of our consciousness? How can we bring children to a place where they can once again lay claim to their innate wonder? How can we help each child participate in discovering the colors of a flower with the enthused wisdom of someone who has not only found a language expressing themselves, but the "wordless" expression of the flower's blues, reds, and yellows?

A possible route is to allow the "nature" of our imagination to become alive once more. To engage children in a process which uses "inner" seeing and imaginative envisioning as much as an ability to see "outwardly." In effect, to make the imaginative bridge between the "nature" we live in and the nature that is ourselves.

To begin with, a simple branch will do. Passing the branch around the room for the children to touch—to feel its subtle contours, its ragged ends, its ingenuous journey—we start talking about where the branch came from and how it might have broken off a tree.

"Do you think this branch felt something when it fell?" I ask the children who by now have "imagined" a life for the branch it did not have when we first started. "What did the tree look like that the branch came from?" I ask further. Almost without hesitation some children tell us by the rustling of their outstretched arms, some with descriptions ("The tree was taller then the room"), and some by drawing on paper their vivid sense of what such a tree may have looked like.

More easily than anticipated, we had reached the imagination. It was in good shape; and even for those children who felt unsure of what to say, its existence was never in doubt. The moment in which children relax into the presence of their imagination there is often a collective sigh of relief—of children smiling to each other, knowing that their inner world is not peculiar to one's self, but a vast gathering of information in everyone, like the richly populated voicing of the sea or a summer meadow. If not specifically articulated there is an intuited understanding that we all now speak the language of the imagination without being criticized. It is the sky each of us lives within.

As we journey, we soon become comfortable watching the tree of our imagination grow. Like us, it moves, gets older, and in its own way, speaks.

My tree is talking to me. She says
'swish, swish', and that means 'oh this
wind is too strong for me'.
And I say to my tree I know what you
mean because I'm feeling it down here too.
—Soo-Jin

> Leaves give the trees ideas—
> and then it pops into the tree's head—
> and then he gives the ideas to all
> the creatures in the forest.
> —*Damien*

> Let it be a beautiful day and let the
> sun and the rainbow come out.
> This is what my tree is thinking.
> —*Stephanie*

To acknowledge the "speaking," the desire to hear and be spoken to by the "inanimateness" of nature, is not an aberration of our minds, but an unerring wish for our world and the world of objects outside to mingle and to hear each other, as portrayed in this Navaho chant:

> Voice above,
> Voice of thunder,
> Speak from the
> dark of clouds;
> Voice below,
> Grasshopper voice,
> Speak from the
> green of plants;
> so may the earth
> be beautiful.

For the imagination to speak—to know that a prerequisite for life is breath—is a step toward the crucial relationship between the "internal" me and the external "it." Nature does not stop at the car or airplane window—or the television screen. Nature is as much the energy and governance of the microchip and the jet engine as ourselves.

The same group of children who began imagining the life of the tree from a single branch were, two weeks later, taken to the park to look at trees. But more than look—to imagine what it might feel like to transform one's self into a tree.

> When I was a boy I tried to be
> a tree and I felt branches coming
> out of my hand and leaves
> coming out of my hand and
> branches coming out of my head.
> I like being a tree.
> —*Bryan*

> This is me and I am a tree and
> I have a mom and dad. It is not
> hard to have a baby when you are a
> tree. You know you are having a
> baby but nobody else does
> because when a tree is having a baby
> a little root comes out to the ground.
> The root that comes out to the
> ground was me and that is how I
> was born. I have aunts
> and great grandmothers.
> —*Jianna*

For children to empathize with the tree's world is to gain an entrance into the "nature" inhabiting us in contrast to the fleeting

appearance of a "nature" distant from us. By using the mythopo-
etic device of "transformation," children became the tree's life. As
Edith Cobb comments in *The Ecology of Imagination in Childhood,* through imaginative journeys children gain a most precious
human way of knowing, "compassionate intelligence." To find
this intelligence is to find the landscape of one's self.

Children's fascination with growth, their own and others,
is a help. To find parallels between their growing and the on-
going reproductive, nurturing, evolving progenies of nature, is
to make the collective entity we know as nature less abstract.
To involve children in outer ecology, we must first involve
them in the "ecology" of themselves. We have to make clear
the stakes they have in making the planet earth livable and sur-
vivable, and what such stakes have to do with the inward landscape of each individual.

A tree is not simply a tree "out there," but the tree each
of us is, metaphorically and biologically. We are dependent on
trees for paper, oxygen, wood, shade, and beauty, and on a
tree's ability to branch within us, as we let it enter as a presence sharing the same biological laws as ourselves. The entry
point is the imagination and its attendant sensory understand-
ings. To be aware of this dialogue is not just a childish desire
but a fact of aliveness—of mutual birth and growth and even-
tual death. It was William Blake who said:

> ...The tree which moves some to tears of joy is in the Eyes
> of others only a green thing which stands in the way. Some
> see Nature all Ridicule and Deformity, & by these I shall not
> regulate my proportions; and some scarce see Nature at all.
> But to the Eyes of the Man of Imagination, Nature is Imagi-
> nation itself.

And Gaston Bachelard echoes in a similar thought:

> The imagination is a tree. It has the integrative virtues of a
> tree. It is root and boughs. It lives between the earth and
> sky. It lives in the earth and in the wind. The imagined
> tree imperceptibly becomes the cosmological tree, the tree
> which epitomized a universe, which makes a universe.

But it is Ted, one of the children from a city classroom,
who, having seen a branch, saw a tree—then himself and his
tree, and who, despite the twentieth–century wizardry of seeing things more quickly and going places faster, gave himself
imaginative moments to listen to:

> When my tree grows its roots grow
> too. Then the tree turned old and
> then it collapsed. But I still see it
> every day. It got its magic by its roots.
> It came from rain.
> It shows its magic by its heart.

The Creatures
They Are

Children Becoming
Their Nature

Not long ago in a classroom in
East Harlem, a group of seven- and eight-year-olds were struggling to put on brightly colored bird masks. With the help of
their teachers, the students tied their masks around their heads.
Beaks securely in place, they spontaneously began to flutter
and dive, chatter and warble, like a flock of newly uncaged
birds. In a moment the usual order of the classroom was transformed by swirling arms and cries.

How could these children capture with such dexterity
and inventiveness so many different qualities of birds?

The hope for this project was to engage the imaginations
of children by letting them become something other than
themselves. If they could imagine themselves as birds, they
could do what birds do—fly, but in this case, fly imaginatively.
We would help create a flock of personal birds as a metaphor
for their own imaginations. The birds would bring them a
deeper awareness of the phenomena of all birds—what they
are, what they do, and what they mean to us.

The children were led through a series of experiences
that brought their imaginative capacities in touch with what

they knew of birds. First, we talked with the children about birds. Yes, they had seen pigeons walking in the park or flying between buildings; they had seen sparrows trailing after the pigeons or washing themselves in curbside puddles; they had heard an occasional crow or hawk or squawking gull. Some children had wondered where birds go when they die; some remembered sighting a nest in the branches of a tree in the park. We asked if they could walk like a bird or imitate the way a bird moves its head when it walks. We asked what they thought feathers do, why birds have colors, how far a bird can see, how a bird flies. The children were quick to offer theories and speculations and took delight in facts; in what they knew and wanted to know.

During this initial conversation, we introduced new ideas. "Do you think there is a bird who could make the rain fall, or who could bring the sun up in the sky?" We asked children to imagine they had become one of those birds, a creator who could do things humans could not. One brave volunteer walked to the side of the room and told us that by moving her arms in a special way, she could bring the night. Another volunteered to make the stars disappear by swallowing them in her mouth. And another made thunder by racing around the room. The transition from what birds were in real life to what birds were symbolically and metaphorically was not difficult.

One day we brought an eagle's feather to class. As we showed it, we spoke of a bird, mysterious and shy, who lurks inside of us. Even as we sleep, this bird roams our thoughts, flying over great expanses of the earth.

We gave the children paper and asked them to draw what they thought this bird of imagination looked like. Secure in their vision, they nestled down into various corners and drew without hesitation their special birds.

When they finished their drawings, we encouraged each child to describe what his or her bird of imagination could do and how it came to be. For most, even those apprehensive about telling stories, there was no shortage of revelations:

> This bird makes everything come alive!
> She makes dead flowers become into alive flowers.
> —*Leola*

> This bird is so powerful that it can turn night into day.
> Its brain is like the brain of a very smart man. When
> he is going to turn night into day it covers the moon
> with his wings and then it makes a very loud sound to
> wake up the sun.
> —*Derrick*

> It was all the colors in the world. The birds grew and
> grew. Every time the bird grows the sun shows more
> light.
> —*Gregory*

> As you know my bird of the imagination is an ancient
> bird and so when it was born it was carved out of rock.
> —*Yeashea*

> The bird of imagination has to get born because if it
> didn't get born, we wouldn't be able to get it out of
> our minds.
> —*Jarrod*

My bird was born from a lightning bolt in my brain.
—*David*

When my bird was in my head, my imagination was bigger. Sometimes the bird would come out and would help me think of something to imagine. How it would do this is it would turn into it. Even when my bird came out no one could see it. But in my head I could. Then I would say what my bird was thinking. And everyone thought I was that smart.
—*Harold*

WIND
The bird shakes around
When the bird shakes round it hurts himself
And then he gets back up and laughs.
—*Safiya*

My bird moves very swiftly throughout the land. It's very special. It has a great home of wonder.
—*Ebony*

The next step was to help the children make masks of their special birds. As a participant in his or her own bird's life, each child could gain a modest sense of what human beings might have experienced on first encountering birds. As the children grappled with paper and paste, they heard how, from the earliest of times, birds were extraordinary presences in the lives of people. How among Native Americans it was Raven of the Northwest Indians who "stole the sun from the chief of heaven and placed it in the sky," and that it was Dew

Eagle of the Iroquois who "carried a bowl of Water on his back and spread cooling dew over the hot earth." And how, according to the Chippewa, "the winds were made by great birds flapping their wings; and the clouds were the wings of the birds hiding the light in the sky."

Connecting children with these traditions strengthens our relation to nature, and the natures we share and that are shared with us. The masks became the children's entryway into a world where the technology of our century had been suspended, and the feel and touch of another species of animal were very much present. Imagination is the mediating element between ourselves and all that surrounds us. As Joel, one of the children in the project, said:

> My bird comes out at night on a full moon. He flies through the sky. At night you can never see him. He is in you. His name is imagination. He lives in a place called heart brain body. It is in everyone. Some adults think it is childish but it will never leave you even if you hide it.

As the school year came to a close in the spring, we wanted to create a ritual to bring the children's imaginative abilities into play with their "birdfulness." One weekend in May, on a day of breezes and new blossoms, we gathered in Central Park—a gift of the city to birds and humans.

Musicians, storytellers, and dancers played, spoke, and danced for us about birds that have flown through human consciousness. The wonder of flight became a possibility. With strips of cardboard and colored tissue paper, the children made wings and decorated them with bright colors. When their wings had been carefully fastened to their arms, our bird troop took to the road in search of the four birds of our imagination—dream, play, transformation, and memory—hiding among the park's bushes and rocks.

Created by four artists, the birds magically came to life at the sound of the children's voices and their flapping wings, to the amazement and applause of the children and their guests. Other birds, high above us, watched from the treetops, as music of a Bolivian flute and drum invited us to follow the final event in the celebration. In a last gesture, we asked crane—another artist's creation, on wondrous stilts—to bring the imagination of the sky to the wings of our birds. We in turn asked our birds to send our imagination, through cardboard wings, back to the sky and to the universe to which we belong.

Tired but elated, the children left the park with their parents and friends. We caught sight of a girl who had separated herself from the others, running hard as she could down the stone path, her cardboard wings with their paper tassels rustling in the wind behind her. In an instant she veered from the path and flew in and out of the bushes and trees, completely unaware of anyone, alive, in the way that animals are, to her own world. Who could distinguish, at that moment, what was bird and what was human? As she flew out of sight with her bird of imagination, she exemplified our human connectedness to living things. In the words of one child:

My thought would be like a bird flying.

The Deep Water
Had
Deeper Fishes

How do we bring imagination to children? How do we make real the imagining process when it is seen as an impractical form of learning? How do we reach the "language of the imagination" when many children have become unsure of their ability to use language for their own feelings and thoughts? What can we do to make the imagination a pivotal force in how children learn rather than a special kind of intelligence, the property only of "gifted" children?

Let us look at the classroom where I am about to speak to public school first-graders on the Lower East Side of Manhattan about creatures of the sea. I start by rustling a few keys that I take from my pocket. I whisper to the children how whenever I take my keys out and listen to the sounds they make in my hand, I am reminded of the sounds fish make as they travel in the darkness of their watery homes. I let my hand move like a fish, wiggling and squirming this way and that—until I notice a few children in the back of the room absorbed in my every movement. I ask one child to take my keys and swim down to the bottom of the ocean with me. By this time the whole class wants to do just that; but before we get everyone involved, I give my attention to Maria, the child standing next to me. I give her the keys—and she wraps them up in her hand. I ask her:

"Would you mind if I took one fish from the keys and let that fish swim with me?"

"No" she replies, handing me one of the fish that she imagines in the set of keys she calmly holds.

"And would you mind if I give one of the fishes to your teacher?" who is standing nearby.

Maria obliges and gives her teacher a fist-full of newly created fish. Now there are three wholesome fish ready to plunge into the ocean. I ask Maria to lead us, step by step, down into the sea. She takes a deep breath (and we take a deep breath too) and gingerly we step into the wet and waiting sea.

Let me pause for a minute because what I have just described is at the basis of the questions I originally asked. We have assumed, as did the children, that "to imagine" is not a difficult task because we started off playing. The keys I jangled in my hand—which I made into fish and the sound of fish— were a quick invitation for the children to play with me. I relied on nothing more than each child's inherent ability for play.

Their acceptance to play and to pay attention to what was in my hand, was their acknowledgement that to play was to invent. A simple household key is only a key until we let our imagination play upon it; then, quite miraculously, it can become a fish, a dinosaur, a walking tree, an upside-down rainfall, or anything at all. Once play has begun, we enter a language, wide ranging as any spoken or written language— perhaps a language which can, if language is our ability to communicate through symbols, out-smart most conventional habits of communicating. For here is a language which can take any object, like a set of keys, and transform it into images. It is a language enabling us to talk to ourselves, through words, feeling, or precise imagery, and often a marvelous blending of all these things. It is a language whose grammar is determined by what we are playing with and how we play; a language which does not speak in ordinary ways, and is often understood only by those willing to listen and respond playfully.

The genius of this language is that no one needs to teach it because it is a child's first language, inherited and made alive through the bones. Its first manifestation is the moment an infant picks up a ball, a stone, or a piece of paper and begins to play. It is the basic language through which children begin to make contact with each other and the "things" of their world.

A child's initial schooling is what he or she learns when this play-language becomes the tool with which to understand. By playing with my set of keys, I translate myself back to a language and a way of knowing that needs little or no introduction to children. It is their willingness to believe that such a language does exist that ultimately makes a difference in how we proceed together.

In this particular first grade, there are a number of children whose first language is not English but who suddenly find an ease of expression and a fluency of thought when we play with our fish. When I ask the children to describe it, there is no end to individual descriptions of long, flat, round, silvery, sharp, and heavy creatures lurking in each child's imaginary realm of the deep.

The children's enthusiasm to tell everything they imagine is a good moment to ask them as a class to draw the swimming creatures. What they portray is not the idyllic waters of a calm ocean but a cross between a benevolent sea and the confused and violent world that many of them must come to terms with in their everyday lives. Some children volunteer the stories and poems within their pictures:

> The guys were running after each other. This guy was fighting with this guy. This is fish water. A fish dies in there. The guy was bleeding. The snake went under the water and the other snake caught him. The other snake jumped up because someone hit him on the head.
> —*Robert*

> My fish slept—and he went far away to the deep water. He went to the pawn shop downtown.
> —*Kristle*

> The shark fell in the water.
> He tried to get the man and the man was moving.
> The turtle is going to bite the shark.
> And then the man is going to bite the turtle.
> The shark said I'd like the turtle to eat him.
> I'm dead 'cause you want to eat me up.
> I love you.
> I love myself.
> —*Molik*

From their drawings on black construction paper, we help them make small cut-out puppets. With these puppets they act out stories, moving them silently through the air as if they, the children, had become the creatures in the depths of unknown waters. Again the language of their play enables many reluctant children to speak and interact with each other. The narratives they bring are the interior worlds that many inhabit but rarely have the opportunity of speaking about to anyone. When we ask the children to share what is happening behind the gestures and movements of their puppets, they tell their story:

> The whale is blind.
> The sun is too hot.
> The kids are playing 'shark-attack.'
> The boat is drowning.
> — *Michael*

> The star is in the earth.
> The air and the star mix up.
> The fish jump into the ocean.
> The sea horse swims in the ocean.
> The man swims in the ocean.
> The man saw the star fish.
> — *Theresa*

Again let us ask how to help children gain access to their imagination, particularly children hampered because they have not mastered the complexities of "correct" language construction. Certainly this is not the case with the first graders who, despite their so-called language deficiencies, find little difficulty in "playing," in "making believe," in "becoming" something other than themselves in order to speak "imaginatively." Their imaginative language is vibrant with a knowledge that contradicts the idea that children who have had little "real-life" experience of the ocean could not "imagine" the ocean. Time and time again, this assumption is proven wrong. They show themselves perfectly capable of understanding beyond factual information.

"Imaginative understanding" is a deeply felt experience and intuition which operates below everyday levels of speech and verbal articulation. It is an understanding within the very fibers of our genetic makeup. It is a language which tries to make sense of who and what we are; a bridge which connects unknowns with knowns, fragments of thoughts with patterns of thought, questions with answers, feelings with actualities. Without this language we would be unable to be aware, to be awake to our own desire to speak, to formulate symbols which make up our daily speech.

If unlocking the imagination with a group of children can happen so quickly and simply by the rustling of keys and my suggestion that fish are swimming inside the darkness of the sea, then we might have a clue as to how to use language with children differently. Perhaps we need, in much of our teaching, to begin with a language of imaginative thought as the basis of how we teach and how children can learn. We ought first to bring children into the metaphors of their own playfulness and, once they are securely inside, allow them to learn from the inside out. (If I am a fish in the sea, what would the water around me feel like, what are the sounds that waves make, what are the colors of the passing daylight?) The questions we ask of ourselves and of children are different when we play, and the answers are that much more personal. If more personal, then language, as a means of explaining ourselves, is less mechanistic, distancing, and closer to being honest and genuine.

Jessica, one child, became so much a part of her own playfulness that she could hardly contain her enthusiasm when I let the fish from my key chain escape into the room each week. Her confidence grew as she entered the language of her imagining and realized how we, her teachers and fellow players, welcomed her thoughts as she drew or wrote about the world within. One day she asked me to sit with her so that I could take down a story. As if reading a book she had memorized, she turned each page of her thoughts with the anticipation of one who savored what came next and knew, instinctively, how important it was for us to be there, listening:

> A mermaid who turned into a woman when she came out of the water.
> And then the deep water had deeper fishes.
> And then the princess star fish came.
> And then the water came over her.
> And then the water turned into a star fish crown.
> And then I came out of the water and lay down next to a giant tree.
> And then the black water came over me when I was laying down over the big giant tree.
> And then the big beautiful rainbow came.
> And then I went in the big beautiful rainbow and I saw a beautiful world.

Being Alive

The
Dancing Child

By chance, a few years ago, I was walking down the hallway of a large urban school when I heard some exhilarating African music coming from a classroom. The hallway was empty except for a child dancing to the music. I suspect he had been on his way somewhere when the music caught his attention and he had to dance. He swayed and turned his arms as if, for a brief moment, he was about to take flight, as if his body, transfixed by the music's rhythms, was obeying a deeper impulse to forget time and place and swirl delightfully onward. As he danced, he assumed a grace and a poise of someone much older and more experienced, giving one the feeling that he had entered into the spirit of the music to such a degree that he was dancing from some awakened ancestral past.

Over the years, I have come back to the image of the child dancing by himself. He has made me think about the impulse within children to respond to feeling by expressing feeling, the impulse, which cannot be taught, to skip when happy, to hum when daydreaming, to giggle when being silly. Uncomplicated impulses, true, but impulses that shape an expression of what is being felt. I'm reminded of a poem by a six-year-old who, when asked how he felt, said:

> I am fainty.
> I am fizzy.
> I am floppy.

These impulses, these origins of responses, lead a child to the initial forms of expression we call the arts. Such responses, found in all humans, from the earliest tapping of stones to make music to spontaneously moving to music's rhythms, are crucial to our survival—crucial because as primary impulses they are the key enabling our interior worlds of feeling and thought to be molded into forms of communication.

The child who danced in the hallway, one hopes, has danced again, so that the impulse that originally moved him to dance has become part of his emerging consciousness, aiding in the expansion of his ability to articulate, aesthetically, the subtleties and contours of his experience. But let his dance also be a reminder of the fragile hold these impulses have in our own lives if they are not nurtured and sustained, if they are seen as infantile expressions rather than the building blocks of a way of life that encourages an individual's right to perceive and understand more fully. As one eleven-year-old child once said to me in his poem:

> Without poetry our world would be locked
> within itself.

Time
Is a Child
Playing

It's summer. School is out. The streets and the parks of New York City have begun to change. Fire hydrants are opened; swimming pools are filled; drinking fountains begin to overflow—and in playgrounds throughout the warming city, sprinklers shower into the air.

For the lucky child a daily visit to one of these sprinklers is not only a way to cool off—it is to challenge the great leaps and boundings of a watery paradise. Some children, too excited to change their clothes, dive in, running through the spray until they are soaking wet. Others, in bathing suits, cautiously approach the surging waters and with their empty hands reach out to feel how strong or how cold this oldest of the elements might be. Like sand pipers, the children dart in and out of the sprinkler's splaying waters, constantly inventing ways to outwit its fluid movements. They squirm and hop, they jump and kick, and then suddenly, as if in prayer, they stop in the middle of a large plume of falling water and, looking up, serenely drink in every moment of its playful wetness.

Sitting on a bench nearby, I feel envious that I cannot

take part in their abandon, their rightful enthusiasm in being a player with the play of water itself. If William Blake is correct and "Energy is Eternal Delight," then what I see is a field of energy, a field of playing in which these children have let go of our all-too-human constraints. They have become, each in their own way, partners in the play of liquid forces which make these waters alive. Perhaps the interplay of the human and the surrounding elements is part of the genius of childhood. To run with the wind, to play with sand and water are not merely idle statements of language, but real descriptions of what a child does when he or she encounters these properties. Through the profound gesture of playing, we enter the life of the wind, sand, and water—or as one eight-year-old child, Johanny, recently wrote, "When I am playing I feel like hugging the wind and kissing and singing with the air, pushing the air far away. I am very, very happy."

For a child, might not the instinctive desire to play also be an unconscious acknowledgment of the play that exists in all forms of nature? As an example, look at any three-year-old alone with a basin of water. In a few minutes, you have a child totally engaged and playing in tandem with the water—teasing, dripping, and splashing, filling and emptying cups, putting in stones and twigs—in short, finding out how the character of water behaves. A playmate has been found in the qualities of water itself, as it responds and reciprocates through the endless variations of its shapes and forms, textures and sounds.

It is no accident that Walt Whitman speaks of "The play of shine and shade on the trees as the supple boughs wag," for he too observes the marvel of playing light as it reacts to the movement of branches—the interplay we see when one element of nature acts upon another. The other day I saw a spider web hanging perilously on the outside of a window. As I looked at it, a slight tremor of air made the web shake, and small dewdrops, almost imperceptible until then, glistened before they disappeared into the morning. Yes, perhaps seeing the web was a mere chance of timing. But as a participating player in this world, can't I also believe in a universe which embraces chance as a primary condition of its play? Much of the world is an improvisation of sorts, an asking and answering, a calling and responding, a movement and counter-movement within processes of nature that invent themselves as they go along, and we within our playfulness are as much a part as the "shine and shade on the trees"—the air touching a spider web—and my eventually being able to speak about it.

Maybe the Greek philosopher Heraclitus was right when he said, "Time is a child playing, moving counters on a game-board: the kingdom belongs to a child." Certainly the children near me in the playground confirm this fact as they rush back and forth into the full force of the sprinkler, encountering the water and finding how it can be shifted and tilted, narrowed and enlarged by sitting on the place where the water emerges. Some succeed brilliantly, letting the weight of their small bodies push the water into submission so that, if only for a few moments, no spray fills the space. They applaud themselves with high-pitched yells and laughter for being masters of the kingdom of waters. But even masters tire of ruling, and with childish spontaneity they quickly run away and let the captured waters go free. In contrast, off in a quiet corner I notice two children funneling dripping water from a broken spigot. Trip after trip, with the diligence of ants carrying dirt to their hills, they ferry precious drops in plastic shovels to the dry desert of the sandbox.

Some of us, commenting on the activity, might conclude that as they play the children are fulfilling the old pedagogical adage, "Play is the child's work." Given the unrelenting attention with which they perform these tasks, this may be true. But I feel differently. The children are also engaged in a reciprocal balancing act between themselves and the work and play of water. For a child, water has a distinct life of its own. To discover this life is to discover the marvel of how water, like ourselves, does things. The writer Laurie Lee, discovering water as a very young child at a pump, remembers how

> ...one could pump it in pure blue gulps out of the ground, and it came out sparkling like liquid sky. It broke and ran, or quivered in a jug, or weighted one's clothes with cold.... It was a plaything of magic, which you could confine or scatter, but never burn or spoil or destroy.

Is the magical playing of water no more than its mechanistic workings, its pre-ordained functioning? Yes, I suspect, if I follow exact scientific reasoning. But if I allow my own reasoning to play, I can ask of play: is it older than us? Did it exist before we did? Johan Huizinga, in his seminal book *Homo Ludens*, states that "play is older than culture, for culture, however inadequately defined, always presupposes human society, and animals have not waited for man to teach them their playing." Might play be the primary condition through which the universe was created? Might the very "work" of the universe be its play? The constant and complex compounding of primary elements to produce life: could this be the same elements at play, risking all in order to multiply themselves into that state of aliveness we know as our world?

I am more at home to say of the waters sprouting from the pavement that they are at play than at work. The latter suggests a seriousness of purpose, a utilitarianism too confining to explain fully the brilliant foliage of light and sounds. If the workings of nature, the invisible dance of its particles holding the universe together, might be its play, then my mind and the children's minds—the mind of the waters, if you could consider it—is nothing less than a vast field of play. Then how extraordinary our playing becomes. Not only does the difficult dichotomy between our "work" and our "play" become meaningless, but our attempts to think, analyze, compose, remember, draw, calculate, dream—to create—are, in themselves, merely marvelous acts of play, at "work" in the deepening evolution of a playful universe.

As I watch the playing children running in and out of the waters, I wonder if we are a translation of a wider field of play. Do we, in our desire to find what and who we are, continue to play, to translate even further, through myths, stories, poetry, and ceaseless questioning, how the universe is teaching us? Will we be able still to hear and see the play of the waters, to feel the urgency of their playing—even after the children have left, the sprinkler has been turned off, the playground is closed, and another warm night settles over the city?

Living
By Wonder

In our grasshopper and salamander days, who among us didn't ask why the grasshopper could jump so far—or why the salamander had black dots on its orange body? We trampled leaves with our feet just to hear what kind of sounds leaves made. We threw flat stones over the surface of streams to see how far the stones could skip. We listened to crickets cry in nights far beyond our grasp of what the darkness was. We slept, only to wake, with the strange sense of how could we be awake when we had only just been sleeping.

In those days we knew as much as we had to know in order to ask what we didn't know. Our ignorance wasn't just innocence but the foundation from which we offered ourselves the daily surprise of discovering another question, another way to uncover something mysterious, something we hadn't understood yesterday. We lived by wonder, for by wondering we were able to multiply a growing consciousness of being alive.

Standing in the doorway in the morning, we wondered at the morning light—and for a brief moment were caught in the stillness of ourselves with everything outside. Yes, we were watching the gathering daylight, but because we wondered about it, it was less a phenomenon we didn't understand than what we wanted to know—a crossing over of what we were and were becoming, to what the daylight was. We stood within another kind of knowledge, a reassuring silence, a nameless warmth, perhaps known and explainable only to ourselves.

In the far north of the Canadian Arctic the young Inuit poet, Panegoosho, begins her poem by saying, "I wake with morning yawning in my mouth"—and continues with, "and I lie still, so beautiful it is, it leaves me dazed, the timelessness of the light." Her wonder, as a way of knowing, transposes our common knowledge of morning so that it is the morning that is waking, yawning, as she boldly states, in the very yawn of her own mouth. She is dazed by the morning's beauty; its light, transposed like herself, is without time—yet is all of time.

Her experience is like what many of us once felt when aware for the first time of how the morning and its light were moving around us. Our wonder, often inarticulate but in clear, translucent feelings, was the means by which we taught ourselves to understand—and, if only fleetingly, gain a foothold on what was there. We were the listening body to our own questions and curiosity, played through us without censorship of ordinary boundaries of reality. For a few minutes we were startled by the life within things—as sky and earth became one immeasurable entity inside us.

The other day my four-year-old daughter, glancing at wildflowers covered in morning dew asked me, "How did all the juices get into the flower?" A question of wonder, in which I sensed one reason we may wonder at all: an insatiable desire not only to know how something is, the very *why* of it, but wanting to know the equally tantalizing *how* of our beginnings, the origin of our own life here. At one point in our lives, we were passionate mythologists attempting to find out how everything came to be: dew, flowers, sunlight, the very earth we stand on. Forged from a deep memory and experience, we created our first myths that explained to ourselves why and how things are and got to be that way. We were makers of that "tissue of wonders" Aristotle called myth, and felt no shame that our ignorance gave us the privilege of inventing the world as we imagined it, asking over and over the necessary questions fed to us by our wonder.

But the life of wonder was short-lived as we got older and encountered other forms of learning imposed by the powerful values of society and schooling. We quickly learned that we cannot succeed, or pass an exam, by wonder alone. We had to go beyond "mere" wonder into the practical demands of the everyday and learn to listen to the logic of a learning that emphasized the rightness and wrongness of what we thought. Retreating from wonder was letting go of a gravitational center within ourselves—gravitational because it nourished the kind of knowledge that may have prompted this eight-year-old child to write:

> This eye started from nothing,
> white tears, sun, tornadoes,
> secrets, night.
> —*Max*

and this nine-year-old to observe:

> The sound
> roaming over me
> breathes steadily.

> The world's breathing
> bringing me under
> swiftly growing
> peace and joy.
> —*Constance*

as well as the archaeologist Jacquetta Hawkes, after a lifetime of researching the origins of humankind, to declare that "we still inhabit a mystery and that the best of scientific wisdom recognizes this is so. Let us have the courage to accept the inner experince that tells us that we are something more—and that we may be part of a process that is something much greater still."

For child or adult the mystery Hawkes speaks of is no less than the gravitational pull of the unknown, the seeming endless spectrum of darkness that, as one child once told me, "can't be solved." Might it also be what Juan Miró was attempting to create in his work when he said, "A pebble which is a finite and motionless object suggests to me not only movements, but movements without end.... What I am seeking, in fact, is a motionless movement, something equivalent to the eloquence of silence"? Or what Miró's fellow countryman, Federico García Lorca, urged:

> Listen, my son, to the silence.
> The undulating silence
> where valleys and echoes slip,
> bending foreheads
> to the ground.
> Listen.

Is this, I ask myself, the silence we hear when we surrender to our wonder? Is it that condition of knowing when we are fully within what we want to know—and, as beholder, are suspended and absorbed between knowing and not-knowing? Is it the silence beneath the poetic experience, as Howard Nemorov speculated, when we become conscious of "the first evanescent flickering of thought across the surface of things...as though the things themselves were beginning to speak"?

Such questions are part of the mystery we must continually accept if we are to remain close to our wonder—unwilling, despite the onslaught of an all-too-measurable and accountable universe, to give up what we knew in the days when grasshoppers and salamanders crossed our path. Days when we stopped and listened, as Basho did some three hundred years ago, when he wrote:

> A chestnut falls:
> The insects cease their crying
> Among the grasses.

For a moment in the mystery of autumnal silence, we are alone with wonder, secure in the knowledge that no matter what else is happening, or what other ways of knowing there might be, the particular language of our wondrous thought is how we interpret what is here. With only this fragile measure of timelessness as our companion, who among us could not now agree with Lao-tsu, who said to us:

> ...From wonder into wonder
> Existence opens.

Credits

I am indebted to the late D. M. Dooling, the founding editor of PARABOLA, and to the various editors and staff at PARABOLA, as well as its present publisher, Joseph Kulin, who, over the course of many years consistently gave me the opportunity to write about those ideas and concerns that have been part of my exploration of the imaginative life of children. The following essays in this book originally appeared in PARABOLA:

> *Making a Language of Childhood* (Fall, 1995)
> *The Wind of the Marigold* (Summer, 1983)
> *The First Question of All* (Fall, 1988)
> *Infant Joy* (Winter, 1987)
> *Trying On a Hat* (Fall, 1994)
> *The Pulse of Learning* (Winter, 1989)
> *Acting Out Daydreams* (Summer, 1982)
> *Emily's Tree* (Summer, 1996)
> *The Speaking of Rainbows* (Spring, 1985)
> *Time Is a Child Playing* (Winter, 1996)
> *Living By Wonder* (Spring, 1997)

I would also like to thank the following journals and organizations where the other essays in this book first appeared:

The Child's Remembering is reprinted, with permission, from *Psychological Perspectives* (Volume 21) © 1989 by the C. G. Jung Institute of Los Angeles, 10349 W. Pico Blvd., Los Angeles, California 90064.

A Season for Listening is reprinted, with permission, from ARTIFACTS (November, 1989), the newspaper for The Arts Council for Chautauqua County, Jamestown, New York.

Suggested Readings

Abram, David. *The Spell of the Sensuous: Perception and Language in a More-than-Human World.* Pantheon, New York, 1996.

Bachelard, Gaston. *The Poetics of Space.* The Orion Press, New York, 1964.

Barfield, Owen. *Poetic Diction: A Study in Meaning.* McGraw Hill, New York, 1964.

Bronowski, Jacob. *The Origins of Knowledge and Imagination.* Yale University Press, New Haven, 1978.

Chung-yuan, Chang. *Creativity and Taoism: A Study of Chinese Philosophy, Art, and Poetry.* Harper & Row, New York, 1970.

Cobb, Edith. *The Ecology of Imagination in Childhood.* Columbia University Press, New York, 1977.

Dissanayake, Ellen. *What Is Art For?* University of Washington Press, Seattle, 1988.

Egan, Kieran. *Primary Understanding: Education in Early Childhood.* Routledge, New York, 1988.

Eiseley, Loren. *The Mind as Nature.* Harper & Row, New York, 1962.

Gardner, Howard. *The Arts and Human Development.* John Wiley and Sons, New York, 1973.

Hawkes, Jacquetta. *Man on Earth.* The Cresset Press, London, 1954.

Read, Herbert. *Icon and Idea: The Function of Art in the Development of Human Consciousness.* Schocken Books, New York, 1967.

Robertson, Seonaid. *Rosegarden and Labyrinth: A Study in Art Education.* Spring Publication, Dallas, 1982.

Rugg, Harold. *Imagination: An Inquiry into the Sources and Conditions that Stimulate Creativity.* Harper & Row, New York, 1963.

Sewell, Elizabeth. *The Human Metaphor.* University of Notre Dame Press, 1964.

Shepard, Paul. *Thinking Animals: Animals and the Development of Human Intelligence.* Viking Press, New York, 1978.

Acknowledgments

M_y sincere gratitude to those many persons who helped make this book a reality, especially to Dr. Monroe Cohen whose wise consul and efforts brought together the first draft of this collection; to my insightful editor at P<small>ARABOLA</small> B<small>OOKS</small>, David Appelbaum, along with his assistant Shanti Fader, who, with much care and patience, edited the present version of the text; to Martin Moskof for the clarity of his design and production ideas; to those dedicated and talented artist-teachers, classroom teachers and administrators with whom over more than two decades, I've had the meaningful pleasure of collaborating in schools; to the various funding agencies and individuals who have generously supported the work of The Touchstone Center; and of course, to those wonderfully alive and inspiring children in classrooms from whom I have learned so much; to my own children, Amanda, Sascha and Sarah—who, with openness and love, have allowed me to share in the richness of their emerging sensibilities; and to my beloved wife, Carol, who always listened with integrity and encouragement enabling me to complete this book with renewed conviction—and confidence.

Index